Inner Simplicity

Inner Simplicity

100 Ways
to Regain Peace and
Nourish Your Soul

Elaine St. James

HYPERION

New York

Book design by Richard Oriolo

Library of Congress Cataloging-in-Publication Data
St. James, Elaine.
Inner simplicity : 100 ways to regain peace and nourish your soul
/ Elaine St. James.—1st ed.
p.   cm.
ISBN 0-7868-8097-X
1. Spiritual life.   2. Simplicity—Religious aspects.   3. St. James,
Elaine.   I. Title.
BL624.S7   1995
248.4—dc20   94-24073
CIP

10 9 8 7 6

To Sam Vaughan and to Wolcott Gibbs, Jr.

In memory of
Phil Babcock
1946–1994

Acknowledgments

M Y SINCEREST THANKS to Marcia Burtt, Catha Paquette, and Pat Rushton for taking their valuable time to read the manuscript, and for their thoughtful comments and helpful ideas.

My deep appreciation to Marisa Kennedy Miller, Jackie Powers, Meg Torbert, Carolyn Howe, Himilce Novas, Dave Sowle, Joe Phillips, Chris Wahlborg, Tiffany Miller, Penny Davies, Frances Halpern, Vera Cole, Chris Souders, Helen Free, Zig Knoll, and Nancy Marschak for rooting, inciting, boosting, exhorting, prodding, promoting, egging, and cheering me onward.

My eternal gratitude to Judy Babcock, Phil Babcock, Jim Cummings, Bev Brennan, and Claudia Bratten for all the inner stuff.

A special thanks to Benjamin Sawyer, Margot Collin, Ken Warfield, Doris Mooney, and all the other reference librarians at the Santa Barbara Public Library who have been so generous with their time and energy, and to all the members of Toastmasters Club No. 5 and Unity Toastmasters for holding still long enough.

I am much obliged to my agent, Jane Dystel, and to my editor, Leslie Wells, and to Laurie Abkemeier, Carol Perfumo, and Samantha Miller for their assistance, encouragement and support, and to Victor Weaver, Marcy Goot, and Brian DeFiore for getting it right.

I am indebted to Anne McCormick and Sam Vaughan for their inspiration and wisdom, and to my husband Wolcott Gibbs, Jr., for everything.

Contents

Two: Easy things to *think* about doing

Three: More difficult things to think about doing

Four: The hard stuff

Five: Some fun stuff

Six: The real stuff

Inner Simplicity

Operating Instructions
for Inner Simplicity:
Read carefully

A FEW YEARS back my husband, Gibbs, and I began the process of simplifying our lives. We'd finally started to realize that we weren't going to be able to do *everything* we'd been trying to do. So we sat down and figured out what we could do and, more importantly, decided what we really *wanted* to do. Then we started, through simplifying, to arrange our lives so we would have the time and energy to do those things that really mattered to us and, for the most part, to let go of all the rest.

We got rid of the clutter in our lives, moved out of our big house into a small condominium, and began what turned out to be a delightful and liberating adventure, which I wrote about in my book, *Simplify Your Life: 100 Ways to Slow Down and Enjoy the Things That Really Matter.*

That process concentrated mostly on the external, or *outer* areas of our lives, such as our household, our finances, our careers, our social lives, and many of the routines of our general lifestyle. The things we did to simplify went a long way toward contributing to happier, healthier, more satisfying lives for both of us. In the bargain, we freed up somewhere between twenty and thirty hours each week to do the things we really wanted to do.

Simplifying the outer aspects of my life gave me the opportunity to discover that there were many areas of my *inner* life that I could simplify as well.

I began to see that there were old conflicts I could now resolve, limiting habit patterns I could change, and new routines I could establish.

I felt that by starting to look within I could simplify my life even more—and increase my physical, mental, and spiritual well-being in the process.

And so I began to explore ways to establish inner simplicity.

What exactly *is* inner simplicity? I've found there is no single answer to that question. It means different things to different people.

For me, inner simplicity means tuning in to what, in my opinion, is the best this world has to offer, such as the love of family and friends, the wonders of nature, and the serenity and clarity that come from silence and quiet contemplation.

It means getting in touch with our creativity and latching on to synchronicity, and figuring out what we need to do to heal ourselves of the things that ail us.

For me, inner simplicity means creating joy in our lives, and remembering to stay connected with that joy every moment of the day.

It means meeting life's challenges, conquering our fears, and letting go of the hurt and the traumas that keep us from being the best we can be.

Inner simplicity means getting rid of the extraneous things—such as worry and anger and judgment—that get in the way of having peace and tranquility in our lives.

It means exploring other levels of consciousness—both the known and the unknown, because I've found that by expanding those levels we can enhance our awareness of how best to live the life we do know.

It also means connecting with a power that is larger than ourselves, whether we think of it as God, a supreme being, or simply the energy of the universe. For some of us, inner simplicity means finding a *middle ground* between the excesses of our outer lives in recent years and the impracticality for most of us of moving to Walden Pond. And so it also means creating an appropriate balance between our inner and our outer lives.

When I thought about it, I realized that my search for inner simplicity had actually started many years ago when I reached the age of reason, which for me was eighteen. It was then I first began to question the beliefs of my childhood (#45).

I spent the next fifteen years exploring various avenues of inner growth, including numerous attempts at learning to meditate (#98), searching for my teacher (#36), working with affirmations (#28) and visualizations (#29), experimenting with diet (#78), studying yoga (#96), practicing deep breathing techniques (#96), exploring various levels of consciousness (#97), and doing lots and lots of reading (#16).

Then, in the mid-seventies, I hopped on the fast track and, for the next fifteen years, with the exception of a couple of forays into the interior regions, left the major part of my inner search on the back burner.

Then, when I'd made significant inroads in simplifying my outer life in the early nineties, and had gotten rid of a lot of the material clutter, the complexities, and the time demands that one collects along the way, I finally came back to taking another look at my inner life.

It was then I began to see that one of my primary motivations for simplifying my life had been to find the time to go within and nourish my soul.

And so I started with some of the things outlined in Chapter Six, such as spending time in solitude, learning to do nothing, tuning in to my intuition, and experimenting with various types of meditation. I wrote about these in *Simplify Your Life*, and I've expanded on them here, based on what I've learned since then.

As I continued, I began working seriously on what I think of as the hard stuff, which I've included in Chapter Four, such as forgiveness, letting go of anger, figuring out my big issue, and getting rid of thoughts that burn.

I tried to balance the heaviness of these things with the more lighthearted aspects of listening to subliminal tapes, casting the runes, chanting, dancing, and creating joy in my life, which I've included in Chapters Five and Six.

And I've continued to find ways to simplify my life, and keep it simple.

Frequently, people who are intrigued by the idea of simplifying but haven't quite gotten to the point of starting to do it yet, ask me, "What do you *do* with all the time you have now that you've simplified your life?"

Inner Simplicity provides some answers to that question. The things outlined in this book are, to some extent, the things I've been exploring since I simplified my outer life and have *had the time* to go within and connect with my inner self.

Obviously, the items included in *Inner Simplicity* are not all-inclusive. There are an unlimited number of other things one can do to achieve inner simplicity. And what appeals to one person may not appeal to the next.

It might be helpful to think of *Inner Simplicity* as a smorgasbord. It includes a variety of things to think about, experiment with, enjoy, reject, pursue, use, take with you, leave behind, or save for another time. There's no hurry, no deadline, no schedule. You can take all the time you need.

Establishing inner simplicity in your life will provide unlimited possibilities for personal growth. It will help you get in touch with how you want to live your life, and give you boundless energy to do it. It will help clear your head and give you a sense of direction and purpose you haven't had before. It will enhance your ability to love yourself and others, and help you create genuine pleasure in every moment of the day. It will give you a new zest for your life and new hope that things can be right in the world.

I urge you to approach inner simplicity as an exciting adventure, a delightful odyssey, a glorious pilgrimage, a wondrous search, a personal exploration, a natural unfolding, and a spiritual quest that has the potential to fill your heart, expand your mind, and lift your soul to new dimensions.

One

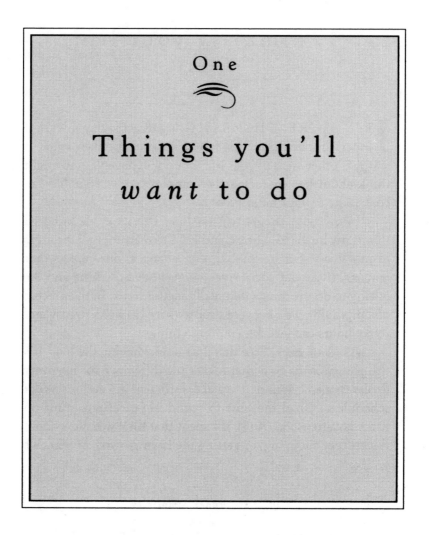

Things you'll
want to do

1. Simplify your life

IF YOU'RE THINKING about achieving a level of inner simplicity, no doubt you've already taken steps to simplify other areas of your life. But if you haven't, you might think about how reducing the complexities of your life can contribute to your inner growth.

In my book, *Simplify Your Life,* I outline one hundred things my husband, Gibbs, and I did to rearrange all the areas of our lives—our household, our finances, our careers, our personal lives, our social lives—so we have the time and the energy to do the things that really matter to us. In the process of simplifying we uncovered somewhere between twenty and thirty hours each week to do those things.

As I look back, I see that it's not just having the *time,* it's the *quality* of the time that makes the difference for my inner explorations. I found it wasn't sufficient to cut my work schedule so I had the time to spend in peaceful solitude on Saturday afternoon (#93), if I spent that time worrying about the grocery shopping, or getting the lawn mowed, or what we were going to take to Jack's potluck dinner Saturday night because I hadn't been able to say no (#54) when he invited us.

You'll find it's much easier to enjoy the full benefits of your quiet time if you're able to reduce the distractions and the energy drains as well.

People often take up yoga or meditation to relieve the pressures of their lives, and to find inner peace. But frequently, unless they've made a conscious effort to make changes in other areas—such as reducing their workload or cutting back on their social obligations—their frenetic lifestyle gets in the way. The inner quest becomes difficult, and it falls by the wayside.

Spend some time thinking about the things you could do to make your life easier.

Simplifying will help create the peace and stability you need to launch into and continue your journey.

2. Spend time each day in nature

MANY CULTURES THROUGHOUT history have thought of nature as an integral and necessary part of their inner lives. Our society, for the most part, has lost contact with the restorative, healing, and inspirational power of the great outdoors.

Make spending time with nature an important part of your spiritual pursuits. If walking is included in your daily regimen, make sure that in addition to the exercise and fresh air benefits of being outdoors, you also connect on an inner level with the beauty of the sun and the sky and the earth.

Start each walk with a deep, invigorating breath of fresh air, and an appreciation of the weather, no matter what it's doing. Make a point of delighting in the trees and birds and flowers and plant life on your route. Let the glories of nature energize your body, heal your psyche, and uplift your spirit.

If you don't exercise outdoors, at the very least make certain you spend a few moments each day appreciating and drawing energy from nature. Plan to leave your house five minutes early tomorrow morning. Before you get into your car or hop on the train, use that time to notice the patterns of clouds in the sky or the dew on the grass. Or, take five minutes before you come into the house when you return from work, and simply acknowledge the closing of another day.

When weather permits, have your lunch outdoors on a park bench, or on the grass under the shade of a tree, and use the time to quietly commune with nature. If the air is clean, do some deep breathing to energize your body and your mind (#96).

Before you go to bed at night, get into the habit of simply opening the front door and stepping outside for a few minutes. Encourage your spouse and your children to join you. You can all enjoy a deep breath of fresh air, and get lost in a silent, meditative look at the night sky.

If you live in the city and are surrounded by tall buildings and concrete, make a special point of taking advantage of nearby parks or nature walks. Be sure your schedule includes weekend trips to places where nature's beauty has been allowed to flourish, and where you can use the power of the cosmos to get in touch with who you really are.

3. Connect with the sun

A LL THE ENLIGHTENED cultures of the past and many sages of the present recognize the role the sun plays in getting us in touch with our soul.

We know our bodies need sun in order to maximize the vitamins and minerals we get from our food. Yet, we now spend close to 90 percent of our time in artificial light.

Numerous studies have shown the debilitating effects on many people of the absence of adequate sunlight. Medical science has recently acknowledged the existence of SAD (seasonal affective disorder), and the need for sunlight for certain personality types.

One of the simplest ways to brighten your mood is to step into the sunlight.

Brief—definitely not extensive—exposure to the sun's rays is tremendously beneficial for our overall physical, mental, emotional health. But most importantly, linking with the sun increases our vitality and elevates our consciousness, thereby contributing to our inner growth.

BARNES & NOBLE
STORE 1878 WESTMINSTER, CO

REG#07   BOOKSELLER#067
RECEIPT#   20190 02/18/96   4:45 PM

S 078688097X   INNER SIMPLICITY
                    1 @   7.95   7.95

SUBTOTAL   7.95
SALES TAX - 7.55%   .60
TOTAL   8.55
CASH PAYMENT   20.00
CHANGE   11.45

BOOKSELLER SINCE 1873

Whenever you can, get ten to fifteen minutes of full exposure to the sun, either early in the morning or later in the afternoon. In winter, sit next to a sunny window to get a mini-sunbath.

Experiment with this. Connect with the sun every day for the next couple of weeks to see how beneficial it can be for expanding your inner awareness.

4. Create beauty in your life

BESIDES TAKING TIME to appreciate the restorative power of the beauty of nature, you'll find it helpful for your inner journey to make your personal environment as uplifting as possible.

This doesn't necessarily mean you have to run out and *purchase* something beautiful. More often, it means getting rid of a pile of clutter or a profusion of objects, each of which has lost its importance because it has become one of the crowd. A single vase on a shelf can have more value and significance to your life than when it's surrounded by a lot of other objects that detract from its singular beauty.

Or it can simply mean creating beautiful empty spaces. I have an artist friend who for years collected valuable objets d'art from other artists and from her travels around the world. Her home resembled a museum, and one practically had to conduct a tour of her living room in order to fully appreciate what each painting or piece of sculpture had to offer.

She recently made the decision to get rid of all of it. She looked around her home one day and realized she no longer knew what she thought because her mind was so distracted by *things*. Not only did they take up space, and not only did she have to worry about their getting broken or damaged, but she had to keep them dusted and lighted and insured. She created a beautiful, contemplative space by letting go of all the objects she had previously thought she couldn't be without.

Take a close look at the things you are surrounded with, both at home and in your workplace. Sometimes we can go for months or years without noticing, at least on a conscious level, some aspect of our environment that is less than pleasing.

Take whatever steps are necessary to make the places you spend your time in as inspiring, beautiful, and liberating for your spirit as possible.

5. Create simplicity, not austerity

WHEN I FIRST started to let go of some of the distractions I had unthinkingly allowed to accumulate in my life and to look within, a friend said to me, "But I don't want an austere life."

I said, "I don't either!"

She had the idea that we were going to give everything away and go live in a hut in the wilderness.

I explained to her that getting rid of a lot of our stuff and moving toward an inwardly simple life is not about deprivation or denying ourselves the things we want. It's about getting rid of the things that no longer contribute to the fullness of our lives.

It's also about creating balance between our outer and inner lives. One of the issues many of us are dealing with now is coming back to our centers after having spent so much time pursuing careers and creating fortunes in the outside world.

We've neglected the inner worlds, and our souls are craving some attention. Devoting more time and energy to the cultivation of our inner lives will help us create that balance and also enable us to live our outer lives more fully.

But living fully doesn't mean having it all, going everywhere, doing everything, and being all things to all people. Many of us are beginning to see that too much *is* too much. Doing too much and having too much get in the way of being able to enjoy the things we *do* want in our lives, and to simply be who we are.

Achieving a level of inner simplicity makes it possible to choose intelligently the things that are meaningful in our lives and that contribute to our happiness and our peace of mind.

It may ultimately mean doing fewer things and having less stuff, but that decision will come, not from self-denial, but from the wisdom that comes by taking the time to figure out what is important to us, and in letting go of all the rest.

6. Learn to enjoy
the silence

I N ORDER TO hear what's happening on an inner level, we have to cut back as much as possible on the external racket. Start becoming aware of the continuously high noise levels you are subjected to every day.

It often begins with the nerve-jangling clamor of the alarm clock, the buzz of an electric toothbrush, or the blast of a hair dryer. This is followed by the drone of the latest news report or the babble of morning talk shows. Then comes the revving of car engines, and the honking of horns in rush hour traffic.

Our days are often filled with the nine-to-five sounds of ringing telephones and office equipment, not to mention the countless interruptions of coworkers, customers, and bosses. Even if you work at home, there can be a constant din from which there is seldom any respite.

On weekends there's the often ear-shattering roar of

lawn mowers or leaf blowers. How can we possibly hear ourselves think?

Often we can't. We're stressed by all the noise in our day-to-day lives—frequently without even being aware of it. At the same time, we're so used to it that it's hard for us to imagine being without it.

As you begin to go within, you'll want to eliminate as much of the outer commotion as possible so you can hear your inner voice.

There may be some noises you won't have any control over—such as traffic or the festivities of neighbors. But you can start by creating as much quiet in your own space as possible.

Learn to wake up without an alarm. Go into your right brain mode (#30) as you're about to fall asleep, and simply visualize yourself waking up at whatever time you choose.

Try going without the TV or stereo for periods of time. Also, leave your Walkman at home when you're walking or exercising, and keep your radio and tape player off, especially when you're driving. Bask in the silence, and use that time to simply be with the moment rather than letting those forms of entertainment distract you from your inner life.

Turn off your phone. Let your answering machine si-

lently pick up messages, which you can listen to at your con-
venience.

Arrange a formal retreat (#95) or a private weekend of
solitude at home (#93) so you can start tuning in to the joy of
silence.

If you haven't been used to it, silence may seem strange
at first, but you'll gradually come to treasure it. Eventually
you'll find it indispensable for your inner search.

7. Have a family meal
in silence

AS A PERSONAL or family ritual, have a meal in silence from time to time. Often the pressures of daily life can make meals a stressful routine. Or we can get so caught up in all the events of the day that we forget to take the time to enjoy our food. The tendency is to hurry through dinner so we can then dash off to the evening's activities.

Sit down with all the family members and discuss how you could approach having a meal in silence. Imagine everyone coming to the table with reverence, and sitting quietly for a few moments while you all connect with each other on an inner level. It's amazing how much you can hear when no one is saying anything.

Rather than mindlessly diving into the food, you could each genuinely but silently express your own gratitude for the meal, and accept on an inner as well as a physical level the benefits of the sustenance it will provide. Then make a point of being aware of the food, and of savoring each bite. So often we rush through meals, talking a mile a minute, and later don't even remember what we ate, or how it tasted.

Obviously there would be no TV or radios or stereos playing in the background. And no reading. Simply contented eating and a true familial connection.

If you have young children, a regular practice of having meals in silence could be an important lesson of family union, and instill in them at an early age an appreciation of the real value of food in their lives.

8. Figure out what you need to do to get well

THERE IS MUCH evidence to indicate that at some level we all have the power to heal ourselves.

Slowing down and learning to look within often makes it possible for us to tap into our own healing powers or, at the very least, find the appropriate healing practice we should follow.

I experienced this firsthand several years ago when I injured my back in a river rafting trip. The range of healing choices available today is mind-boggling. I had lots of people suggesting lots of different methods of treatment.

Fortunately, I'd spent the previous couple of years simplifying my life and had started, for possibly the first time ever, to listen to my inner voice. After a six-month process of trial and error, I connected with the ancient healing technique of acupuncture that virtually healed my back in a couple of weeks.

This is not to say you should ignore the options of modern medicine, some of which can provide almost miraculous cures for what ails us. But, whenever possible, take the time to *listen*.

Consider *all* the options. If you've got an ailment or an injury from which you are not recovering, look into self-healing or alternative methods of healing and repair, such as visualization and positive imagery, especially if traditional medical treatments you've been using aren't working. Standard medical practices tend to focus on symptoms and disease rather than on health and wellness. Often the cure is worse than the illness.

I know listening to an inner voice isn't always easy. I spent six months virtually flat on my back in continual pain and discomfort, essentially incapacitated and unable to live a normal life. And, in the first six months or so, nothing I did seemed to help.

Even though my problem wasn't life-threatening, it was frightening and discouraging to feel there was no end in sight. The temptation was strong to take what seemed at the time to be the easy way out, and pursue what could ultimately have been a disastrous course of surgical treatment. In the past, I might very well have done that. Now I waited, and listened.

In time the appropriate solution for my situation came.

We each know exactly what we need to do to heal ourselves. If the circumstances are appropriate, make it your personal quest to spend time in solitude or quiet contemplation until your intuition guides you to the proper course of treatment or self-healing.

9. Get in touch with your creativity

WE'RE ALL BORN with a deep core of creativity. Some fortunate few are able to connect with that core at an early age. Others of us spend years longing, oftentimes unconsciously, to tap into it. Many of us go through life denying that it exists. We live with the belief that we are not creative.

Often there are explanations we can point to that justify our seeming lack of creativity. Possibly it was stifled through some childhood trauma, or by real or imagined criticisms from our mentors. Maybe it was simply starved by the absence of encouragement when we needed it.

Like many people, I grew up believing I wasn't creative. At some level I recognized that this denial excused me from having to *try* to be creative. I also recognized that *saying* I wasn't creative kept me from *being* creative.

At another level, however, I wanted to explore the artistic possibilities. Over the years I've enrolled in dozens of art and drawing classes, hoping to learn to draw and paint. Over and over again I would drop out of these classes after just a few sessions because I was embarrassed to be the only one— or so it always seemed to me—who couldn't draw. Perhaps you've done this, too.

Julia Cameron, in her wonderful book *The Artist's Way* says this is analogous to dropping out of a French class because we can't immediately speak French. But this is a common occurrence. Many of us have come to believe that if we weren't born with talent, we'll never be able to develop it.

High on the list of major benefits I've received from inner simplicity has been the ability to get in touch with my artistic side. Some months after I'd started meditating (#98) and almost immediately after I'd completed some serious work on forgiveness (#70), I was able to start painting.

And because I'd started to learn through meditation that it's all right to just *be*, I felt okay with just being a *bad* painter. That got me to the point of being an okay painter.

For many of us, the ability to tap into our creativity comes only after we have slowed down to the point where we can take the *time* to get centered. Learning to *be* and learning to be creative are two sides of the same coin. Now that you have the time, your inner search can open you up to both.

10. Latch on to synchronicity

W E'VE ALL HAD days where everything just seems to go right. We hit the traffic at the opportune moment, and drive straight to the office without delays. We pull into the parking lot just as a convenient parking space opens up for us. The people we've been trying to reach all week suddenly call or appear, and we're able to wrap up our business with them with unusual efficiency. Our iced tea is cold and our soup is hot. The money comes out of nowhere for a project we want to start. Everything is in sync.

Since I've begun taking steps to simplify my life—both outer and inner—I've found synchronicity operates in all areas, and much more frequently than it did when my life was complicated. Over and over again, as soon as I've become clear on what it is I want, the circumstances I need to get it are miraculously available to me.

As I look back, I realize that before I slowed down, the

messages and the possibilities for these synchronicities had always been there, but often I was too busy to pay attention to them, or didn't believe them when I heard them.

This is not to say that *everything* is now a piece of cake for me. But I've learned that if things aren't going well, I need to slow down and listen. When I get back into sync, things start to flow again.

Reducing your pace and looking within will help you make your life work the way you want it to. It will also expand your time and energy so that synchronicity becomes a natural and joyous part of your life.

If you like the idea of latching on to synchronicity, perhaps it's time to make a formal declaration to yourself and the universe that this is what you want. It's amazing what can happen when we simply declare ourselves in the game.

11. Slow down

I WAS SURPRISED to discover that simplifying my life didn't automatically mean that I'd slowed down, too. The speed of life on the fast track permeates every area of our lives. Hurrying becomes a *habit*. Even after we've simplified many of our daily routines, if we're still surrounded by fast-moving people and phones that never stop ringing, slowing down can take a major effort.

Start by thinking about how you can slow down your morning routine. Getting up even half an hour earlier so you won't have to rush out the door will make a big difference in the pace of your entire day.

Take the time to *sit down* for your morning meal. Eat in a leisurely manner so you can feast on each bite. Eliminate the distractions of the radio, TV, and morning paper. Simply enjoy eating.

Make the gathering, preparation, and consumption of

food a conscious part of your inner quest, especially if you have lunch or dinner in fast-paced restaurants away from the peace and quiet you have established in your home. In fact, as much as possible, avoid fast-paced restaurants for your mid-day meal. Have your lunch on a park bench in the sun or sitting on the grass in the shade.

Plan to leave home in plenty of time so you don't arrive at the office panting at the start of your workday. If possible, walk to work, or take the bus or some other form of public transportation so you won't have to compete in rush hour traffic. If you do drive, make a point of staying within the posted speed limit. Learn to appreciate moving with purpose at a leisurely pace.

Place Post-it notes around your home or office to remind yourself to *slow down*. Over and over I found that rushing through a project meant getting it wrong and losing time in the end by having to do it over, either partially or completely. Take your time and do it right in the first place, and *enjoy the process* as you go along.

Make a concerted effort to examine all the areas of your life, and figure out where you can slow down. If you've simplified a lot of your daily and weekly routines, you now have more time. Use some of it to reduce your overall *pace* of life so you can derive more pleasure from each thing you do throughout the day.

Slowing down will help you keep in touch with how you feel about what you're doing, and make it easier to connect with your inner self.

12. Learn to receive

YEARS AGO I studied hatha yoga with a wise woman who taught the art of *receiving*. We learned to take the time necessary to complete each yoga position, and then to take the time it took to *receive* the benefits of it. It was an invaluable lesson, and one we can incorporate into every area of our lives.

Get in the habit of *receiving* the benefits of the things you do. When you come in from your walk, take a few moments to *absorb* the contribution the exercise and the fresh air have made to your day and to your life.

When you finish a meal, sit still for a moment and be *conscious* of the benefits the food brings to your body.

When someone pays you a compliment, instead of shrugging it off, accept it fully into your being, even revel in it. When you do something thoughtful for someone else, enjoy not only the pleasure they may derive from it, but the satisfaction it gives *you* to perform a good deed.

When you complete a project, take some time to *ac-*

knowledge your accomplishment before you rush off to begin the next one.

So many extraordinary things happen to us throughout the day and throughout our lives. We often either ignore them or make light of them as though they were unimportant. They *are* important. Take the time to notice them.

The little things may take only a moment or two to acknowledge. All you have to do is stop for a couple of minutes, and *receive*. You'll know when you've taken it in completely, and when it's time to move on.

For the bigger things, like the completion of a work transaction or the achievement of a major goal, schedule whatever time you need to totally embrace the contribution you have made and *receive* the benefits of it.

Now that you've simplified your life, you have the *time* to assimilate into your being the synchronicities, the beauty, the love, the joys, and the work of your day. As they happen, let their beneficence pour over you and penetrate every fiber of your being.

In a very real sense, these daily events make you what you are. Indulge yourself. Enjoy them. Receive all the amity they have to offer.

13. Be realistic

W HEN WE FIRST made the decision to start simplifying our lifestyle, Gibbs and I sat down and made
a list of our priorities. Our first list included twenty to thirty
things we wanted to concentrate on.

As we moved along in our plan to simplify, we began to
see that even after we had taken some major steps to free up
our time and energy, there was no way we'd be able to do *everything* on our list.

So we cut back and ended up, at least for starters, with
four or five things that were most important to us: our marriage, our writing careers, spending time with family and special friends, and pursuing our personal hobbies of reading and
exploring cultural pursuits.

In one respect that doesn't seem like much—at least not
compared to what we *thought* we wanted to do, or compared
to what many of us have been *trying* to do. But if you've got a
spouse, and children, and a career, and certain responsibilities
you *can't* get out of, three to four priorities is about all you

get. There's really not a whole lot of time for anything else, especially if you want to include quality inner time as well.

Recognize that inner pursuits take time, too. And to get the maximum benefit from going within, that time should be free of the distractions and the complications we often allow our lives to be full of.

So as you start to make changes in your life and in your schedule, be realistic. Attempt to strike a balance between your outer and your inner goals, and keep in mind you may not be able to do *everything* you think you want to do.

14. Figure out what you *don't* want in your life

IN ADDITION TO figuring out what your priorities are, it is also helpful to figure out what you *don't* want in your life anymore. This is a subtle distinction, but it's an important one to make.

We allow a lot of mental, emotional, and psychological clutter to accumulate in our minds and our lives, blocking our access to inner peace.

This clutter includes doing things we don't want to do but continue to do, either because we said we'd do them or feel we *should.*

It includes spending time with people we no longer want to spend time with because we've outgrown the relationship or because they don't contribute to our inner growth.

It includes doing work we aren't happy doing.

It includes trying to do too many things, even if a lot of them are things we do want to do.

It includes not doing enough of the things we want to do.

It includes engaging in idle gossip and meaningless chatter that drains our energy and leaves us feeling grungy.

An amazing amount of the clutter includes fuming over past events we can't change, or being distracted by future events that may never happen. It includes judgment (#65), and harboring thoughts that burn (#62).

As you move toward developing harmony in your life, you'll find a lot of this stuff will fall by the wayside. Some things, however, will require an effort on your part to make sure they are eliminated.

You might want to sit down with your journal (#31) in the next few days and make a list of the things that are getting in the way of your inner progress. Then set up a plan to get rid of them.

15. Enjoy each moment

O NE OF THE ultimate objectives of attaining inner simplicity is learning to live happily in the present moment. Keep in mind that life is a continuous succession of present moments. Most of us spend an inordinate number of our moments regretting the past, or fidgeting in the present, or worrying about the future. We miss a lot of life that way.

Worry and regret and being anxious are *habits* that keep us locked in old patterns. But these habits can be eliminated once we've become aware of them.

If you find such habits are getting in the way of being happy, think about what you can do to change them. It sounds simplistic to say it, but you can get into the *habit* of enjoying your life. Setting up a calendar and a box of stars is one way to approach building this habit (#61).

Another way to choose to enjoy each moment is to start taking responsibility for your life (#68). If you're not happy in your present circumstances, you have no one but yourself to blame. Make whatever changes you need to make so that you *are* happy.

Going within will automatically bring you to a level of enjoyment of your day-to-day life that you may not have experienced before. Making the conscious effort to enjoy each moment will make your inner quest that much easier.

16. Take time to read

THERE ARE THOSE who say that once we get far enough in our inner journey, we'll know everything we need to know from a deep awareness of our own experience.

In the meantime, for those of us who are still plodding along, the appropriate books are an invaluable source of information, inspiration, courage, insight, advice, and confirmation that we're headed the right way.

Keep a suitable selection of books on your bookshelves, by your desk, in the glove compartment of your car, next to your favorite easy chair, and anywhere else you find yourself on a regular basis.

Whenever you start to worry, or feel sorry for yourself, or feel lonely or depressed, or find that you're judging others, or thinking negatively, or feeling anger or resentment, pull out a relevant book.

The list of soul-nourishing literature is almost endless. At the back of this book I've included a list of some of the works I've found helpful.

17. But don't read in bed

ALL MY LIFE I've read in bed until lights out, so I know this will sound like heresy to those who love to read themselves to sleep. But once I started to explore other levels of awareness, I found that reading just before sleep was a major distraction.

When I thought about it, I realized that often I was simply too sleepy to adequately absorb what I was reading, and frequently I'd have to go back the next day and spend time reading the same material over again. Or I'd fall asleep in the middle of reading about someone else's life drama, and would end up tossing and turning with wild and fantastical dreams that didn't contribute to my sleep or my life.

My friend Margaret mentioned to me recently that she'd been having nightmares. Since I'd just begun to explore my own dreams, I asked her if she had changed her bedtime routine. She assured me she hadn't; she was reading until she fell asleep, as she had always done.

It turned out that her favorite aunt had recently sent her

a huge box of detective stories that she was clearing out and thought Margaret would enjoy. The problem was that Margaret did enjoy them, which is why it took her some time to figure out that reading them just before sleep was having a negative impact on her dreams.

For a while, I made a practice of keeping only uplifting or spiritually oriented reading material on my nightstand. But after experimenting, I've found it's better to fall asleep consciously than under the influence of someone else's psyche, no matter how elevated it might be. This is especially important if you're exploring your sleep consciousness (#97).

I've gotten into the habit of having a few moments of quiet reflection or possibly even a brief meditation just before going to sleep. This has contributed significantly to my inner simplicity.

For the next few weeks, try going to sleep without reading in bed. You'll notice a big difference in your moods, in your intuitiveness, and in your level of awareness. You're also much more likely to get a good night's sleep.

18. Sleep a lot

SLEEP IS A vital part of your inner growth, especially in the early stages. There is a lot going on at the sleep level of consciousness that we are only just beginning to understand. Many spiritual retreat programs include naps, rest time, and/or sleep as a major part of the daily regimen.

If you've been moving quickly on the fast track in recent years, you may desperately need sleep to restore your body and your mind, not to mention your psyche. If you've simplified your life, you'll have time now to sleep and still do many of the other things you may want to do.

So sleep in whenever you can. Go to bed early every night for as long as you need to. Sleep throughout the weekends. Take naps whenever possible. Relish sleep. Luxuriate in it. Grow in it. Expand in it. You need it.

Two

Easy things to *think* about doing

19. Have weekend retreats at home

I F YOU'RE WORKING on establishing a level of inner simplicity, few things you can do will give you a better boost than a formal retreat (#95). But if you're not quite ready to do that, or you can't take the time now, arranging your own retreat at home might be the next best thing.

Obviously, having a weekend retreat at home will be easier if you're single or if your spouse and/or children are either away for the weekend or receptive to the idea of your taking some time on your own.

Set aside your normal weekend routine. Plan to start your quiet time by dinner on Friday evening and carry it through Sunday evening. Unplug the phone, and tell your family and friends that you won't be available until Monday morning. Plan not to answer the door.

Turn off your TV and your radio; put newspapers and magazines away, but make certain you have a supply of appropriate reading materials (#16). Take your watch off so you are not concerned with time. Wear loose-fitting comfortable clothes. Avoid the type of food and drink or other substances that will lower your energy.

Do whatever you need to do to your space to make it as pleasant and as conducive to quiet reflection as possible. Air out the rooms; bring in fresh flowers; provide candles or incense or essential oils. Have everything you might want at hand so you won't have to dash out into the world.

Spend your time in silent reflection. Meditate. Do yoga or gentle stretching. Practice deep breathing (#96). Write in your journal (#31). Create your inner affirmations (#28) and visualizations (#29), and start practicing them. Watch sunrises and sunsets. Take a mini-sunbath to keep your mind and spirits elevated. Spend time in nature. Stroll in the early morning or evening, away from people and traffic. Sit quietly, not thinking, just being with the moment. Ask for guidance and be open to whatever messages come to you from the universe.

Go to bed early and get up with the sun, or even earlier. If you rarely get to experience the joy of the birth of a new day, this is a good time to start.

Prepare your meals with love and awareness. Eat in silence without reading or any other distractions; make a point of savoring each bite.

Make a commitment to yourself not to worry or to engage in negative thinking during this time. If necessary, use the bean system (#63) to become aware of your thought patterns. If you feel lonely or frightened, write about your feelings in your journal.

This is the time to reconnect with your soul. Enjoy it.

20. Consider a family retreat

IF YOUR FAMILY is amenable, consider spending a silent, meditative weekend retreat at home together. This can be a very powerful and effective way to strengthen the family bond.

If you haven't already established a pattern of regular times of solitude with your family, a retreat—even a quiet, contemplative afternoon together—would be a good way to start.

21. Remember, growth isn't always a family affair

ONCE YOU START to look within and experience new insights about the world and your place in it, it'll be only natural that you'll want to share them with your family.

Consider yourself fortunate if the other members of your household are ready at the same time you are to explore the inner realms. It's much more likely that you'll be ready, but your spouse and your children won't be. Be prepared for this possibility, and don't make an issue of it. They'll come along when the time is right. Or they may not.

If you find yourself in this position, spend some time sincerely listening to your inner voice (#92). Figure out how you can move forward on your quest without alienating your family. Your task will be to arrange your life so you can continue your inner explorations without making anyone else feel uncomfortable or threatened.

How you proceed will depend to some extent on the level of communication that has already been established. Go slowly, and don't be attached to having them join you. It may be that the most you can hope for is their understanding and acceptance.

If you can't get even that for the moment, learn to keep your own counsel (#72), and don't make anyone else wrong in the process. Learning to deal with the reactions of the people close to you could be a major part of your growth. Your biggest challenge may be to accept the situation as it is, and continue on your way.

22. Don't get caught in the righteousness of your path

WHILE I'M FORTUNATE that Gibbs has been totally supportive of the inner explorations I have pursued in recent years, his methods of connecting with the soul have been quite different from mine. Happily, we've been able to establish a relationship in which we can each follow our own inclinations, respect each other's choices, and share with each other what we're learning.

But no matter how comfortable we are with our diverse paths, part of me wishes we were both on the same path. Namely mine, of course.

Recently, we took our own private retreat together at a favorite spot of ours in the mountains. He did his thing, and I did mine. After several days of quiet contemplation we found ourselves sitting side by side. I was reading about zen meditation; he was reading a biography of Napoleon.

Finally, I decided to ask him a question that had been

on my mind since I had begun this process of looking within.

So I turned to him and said, "Do you think I'm more evolved because I'm doing all this searching? Or are you more evolved because you aren't?"

He pondered this for a quiet moment, then said, "Maybe we're both evolved, but we're just expressing it in different ways."

I had to acknowledge the wisdom of this response. And it gave me the chance to see that at some subtle level I had been feeling smug about the rectitude of my inner work.

As we discussed it further, I also had to consider the fact that being *evolved* had nothing to do with it—we're both simply doing our own thing. It's so easy to fall into the trap of thinking that the inner quest is somehow superior to the activities of the everyday world. But inner seeking is just inner seeking. There's nothing inherently better about it. Outer explorations are just as necessary and just as valuable. The inner stuff often *seems* more important to those who are in the midst of it because many of us have spent so much more time recently in the marketplace and so little time cultivating our own souls. When our lives are in balance, there is no distinction between the outer and the inner.

This is a good lesson for me to remember. And remember. And remember.

I share it here in case you might need to remember it at some point, too.

23. Form a support group

THE INNER SEARCH requires a lot of time alone when you may well be doing things differently from the way you've been doing them. It's possible many of the things you'll be doing will be different from what most people you know are doing. You'll no doubt be having new insights and revelations about your life and your purpose. Sometimes it'll be exhilarating; sometimes it might well be terrifying.

And sometimes it will seem as though nothing at all is happening. You may find it helpful to be in touch with people who have some conception of what you're going through, and who have been there themselves.

Recently I spent several years in a group of three women and two men who were committed to inner growth. Our weekly meetings provided a safe setting where we could freely discuss the changes we were experiencing on a metaphysical level. The progress we made together not only elevated the energy of the group, but contributed to each of us individually.

Keep your eyes open and put feelers out for people who might have similar goals and interests to your own. These need not be people you know or are currently friends with. People who don't know you are sometimes more likely to be objective when it comes to evaluating your situation and your progress.

If you haven't experienced the tremendous benefits that can come from participating in a small group of people who are dedicated to each other's growth, I urge you to think about how this might enhance your inner work. You may have already discovered that the people you most want to spend time with are those who are working at the inner levels, too.

Eventually, it's likely you'll have to step into the void on your own, but until you reach that point, surrounding yourself with like-minded people can help you create an atmosphere for real spiritual transformation.

24. Create a positive structure for your group

W HEN WE FIRST set up our inner group, we found it helpful to agree on some guidelines for how our meetings would be structured.

We decided to meet at the same time and at the same place every week, and we each committed to the group and to each other for at least six months. We felt we would need at least that much time to establish a real bond of trust, and to get a feel for how effective these meetings would actually be.

As it turned out, the process was so helpful for each of us that we continued to meet weekly for several years, until a couple of the members moved out of the area.

In terms of format, we tried various approaches and decided what worked best was to allow each person half an hour or so to share whatever they felt was appropriate about their inner progress from the previous week, or about any new insights they might have come up with.

Then we took time for comments and suggestions from the other members before going on to the next person. We started the meeting with a different person each week.

We found that every now and then we needed to change the format of the meeting in order to adapt to the particular circumstances of the members. If one of us was at a critical juncture and required more time, other members would give up their time to the person who needed it most that week. We each knew we would get it back when our day of need came.

We decided not to bother with refreshments. We didn't want any outside distractions.

We also agreed that anything we discussed would be confidential.

We selected a meeting place where there were no spouses or children who might interrupt, and the host agreed to turn off the phone while our meetings were in progress.

If you're putting together a group of people who are dedicated to inner development, take some time in the beginning to arrange a format that will work for the members and for the group as a whole. Then be open to changing the structure as the group evolves.

25. Have some fun while you're at it

EVERY NOW AND then, we changed the format of our inner group meeting entirely. Once, one member brought blankets and food, piled us all into his Jeep, and drove us to the top of a local mountain peak. We had a very high-energy meeting in the cool night air as a beautiful full moon rose over the valley.

Another time we drove down to the beach and romped through the crashing breakers in the dark of night. Then we built a fire on the beach, and had a group meditation.

Once we arranged to spend a day on a wilderness adventure course. We confronted our own fears or limitations with rock climbing, rappeling, tree climbing, and nature hikes.

All these things were done with the intention of elevating our consciousness so we could team up with each other and with our higher selves through nature. We created a special bond individually and as a group that immeasurably helped our future work together.

Connecting with a group of like-minded people on an inner level can provide many benefits, not the least of which is to remind ourselves that our inner search can be fun as well as challenging.

26. Monitor the obvious distractions

IF YOU'RE MOVING toward inner simplicity, you're probably already cutting back on many of the diversions that may previously have occupied a lot of your time, such as television, movies, videos, noisy bars, and crowded restaurants.

You may find that the entertainment aspects of the inner realms are not only much more satisfying, but they leave you feeling refreshed and rejuvenated, whereas many of the more popular gratifications deplete your energy and often bring you down.

This is not to say that any of these amusements are unacceptable in themselves, or that you want to eliminate them entirely. But if you think about it, you can figure out which activities you might have partaken of in the past, that now no longer contribute to your well-being or your peace of mind.

And, if you think about it some more, you can come up with activities—sometimes seemingly insignificant ones—

that can fill your soul. A while back I was washing some grapes for lunch. I looked at that bunch of big, red, luscious grapes and saw how exquisitely beautiful they were. It was almost as though I'd never seen a grape before. I held them up and turned them this way and that and marveled at the gradations of color and how they appeared to change shape as the light hit them.

I stood for some minutes, totally absorbed in the essence of those grapes. And in those few moments I sensed my whole awareness expanding. I felt full to the brim, and I hadn't even eaten the grapes yet! I'm sure I got more sustenance from looking at those grapes than from any of the movies I've seen in recent years.

You may think spending an evening watching a bunch of grapes is not your thing. But if you're looking to feed your spirit, it might be preferable to watching people machine-gun each other into oblivion. If grapes don't do it for you, think about sunsets, sunrises, moonrises, moonsets, stargazing, or simply staying home and playing Scrabble with your kids.

You may also find yourself going through periods of time when nothing is coming through on the inner channels. That's when you can do something like casting a rune (#86), or dancing (#91), or chanting (#90), or laughing (#59), or possibly crying (#84).

27. Create your own sanctuary

IT WILL BE important for your inner pursuits to have a space you can call your own. It could be your own room, or even a small corner of a room. It will be somewhere you can go and not be disturbed.

This will be where you'll meditate, contemplate, do nothing, think, read, heal yourself, enjoy the silence, and do your journal writing. You can do your affirmations and visualizations here. You can keep your discipline calendar and your box of stars here (#61). You can review your day here (#41). It'll be a very functional space. Do whatever you need to do to make it special and sacred.

I have a huge cozy armchair in a corner by a window. I can sit comfortably for reading, and straight and alert for meditating. I keep a stack of my favorite books by the chair.

I have a tape player nearby where I can listen to my subliminal tapes or to music that I find uplifting—though usually I just enjoy the silence. I know I can go there at any time to clear my energy, or to work out a problem, or to just sit quietly and BE. Gibbs knows not to interrupt me when I'm there.

If you've never had the luxury of a place where you can go on a regular basis to get away from the daily routine of your life and be alone, don't waste another moment. This space will be essential for your spiritual growth.

28. Use affirmations

A N AFFIRMATION IS a mental or verbal declaration to yourself and to the universe about how you
want your life to be. Words and thoughts are powerful things.
Your life as it is right now is a physical manifestation of all
your thoughts, both positive and negative.

Positive affirmations are an effective tool for clearing the
negativity out of our minds and our lives, and for propelling
us along in our efforts to create our lives exactly the way we
want them to be.

I've used affirmations for years in my personal and business life. Anyone who has used them consistently knows how
effective they can be in helping us to achieve what we want in
our lives. But I was well into my inner search before it dawned
on me that affirmations could be effective there as well.

Take some time in the next few days, either on your own
or with an appropriate book, to come up with a personal statement that expresses the thing or things you most want in your
life right now—peace, tranquility, simplicity, wisdom, en-

lightenment, omniscience, spiritual growth, whatever.

Make your affirmation a positive statement that declares to yourself and to the universe that you have this thing or quality in your life right now, such as "I live a simple, peaceful life."

It doesn't matter if the statements you affirm are not true yet. Repetition of an affirmation, combined with *belief* and *imagination,* enhances the ability of your subconscious mind to bring about the reality you affirm.

Use a section of your journal to record these affirmations for your daily use. Get into the habit of actively thinking about and repeating selected ones to yourself throughout the day. Use Post-it notes or whatever means works as a reminder until the habit of working with your affirmations for your inner growth is firmly established.

Then be prepared to change and/or adapt your affirmations as your life changes, and you gradually begin to become the things you affirm yourself to be.

I've included several books in the Reading List that are helpful for understanding, creating, and using both affirmations and visualizations.

29. Use visualizations

HAND IN HAND with affirmations go visualizations. In addition to verbalizing to yourself both silently and out loud the inner qualities you want to develop, creating a powerful mental image that projects how you want your life to be focuses your attention on that outcome and helps bring it into your life.

Numerous studies in recent years have shown how effective visualization can be for healing, personal growth, and empowerment. Like affirmations, visualizations are just as potent for our spiritual journey.

Spend some quiet time in your sanctuary thinking about how you would look and feel to yourself if you had the inner qualities of love, compassion, joy, gratitude, understanding, patience, tolerance, acceptance, or whatever attributes you seek.

Pick one trait, such as compassion, and step into it each morning as part of your daily routine. Make this a habit. In your mind's eye, actually *see* yourself having this quality.

Imagine how you would look and how you would feel if you had compassion. Check with yourself throughout the day to make sure this feeling of compassion is still with you. Do this until you've absorbed this quality. Then move on to the next one.

We are continually bombarded with negative messages that can easily deflect us from our search for inner peace. Developing the ability to counteract that negativity with positive mental images will go a long way toward keeping you on track.

30. Use your right brain mode

MUCH RESEARCH HAS been done in recent years on the various levels of the mind, particularly the right brain mode, or the alpha level of consciousness, where we can tap into our creativity, get in touch with our intuition, enhance our thinking processes, and improve our performance in sports and other activities, among many other things. This is the level of the mind where artists, writers, and all great thinkers get their ideas. It is where we all work on problem solving and the creation of new perceptions and understandings.

Years ago I took a Silva Mind Control Seminar in which we learned how to create a "workshop" in our mind at the alpha level. We simply relaxed into the right brain mode and, using our imagination, created a space in our mind's eye where we could go to work on problems of any type at the alpha level.

We learned to clear up headaches, find lost objects, and even get rid of infestations of ants! (Anyone who has tried these methods knows how effective they can be. Skeptics can continue to use Raid.)

The theory is that any information we need to do the work we want to do is available to us. We simply have to get into the practice of tapping into it.

You may already be using these techniques in your life. If so, think about how you might use them for your inner endeavors.

One of the things I did almost unconsciously when I started to go within was turn my workshop into an "inner sanctum." Now I do almost all my inner work there. It's where I listen, heal, create affirmations, enhance visualizations, and do my serious thinking, among many other things.

If you're not familiar with right brain techniques, you might want to check out some books that outline detailed methods for accessing other levels of consciousness. Several are suggested in the Reading List.

Going into the alpha level is very easy to do. One technique is simply to sit down, close your eyes, relax, and take a couple of deep breaths. Breathe quietly for a few minutes. You might find it helpful initially to count backward slowly from ten to one. You'll begin to recognize a slight shift in your level of awareness, and you'll know you're in the right brain mode. Being effective there happens by *intention* and *imagination*.

After you've done this a few times, you'll recognize the *feel* of the space and how to get there, and you can come and go at will. It is a safe and very powerful place for your inner operations.

31. Expand your journal

I HAVE USED a journal on and off over the years for recording dreams and for writing about personal issues as well as to help me sort through difficult or complicated situations.

Since I simplified my life and have started my inner search, I've expanded my idea about what a journal can be. It has actually branched into a spiritual workbook. I've found it an invaluable tool for keeping track of my thoughts and feelings, and for recording the progress of my quest.

Now, in addition to sections for dreams and journal writing, I have space for recording affirmations and visualizations, since these change on a regular basis as I adapt them to my needs.

I have a section for recording rune readings (#86), since this is such an effective way to stay in touch with and develop my intuition. It's been helpful to be able to refer back to see how the runes have guided me in the past on a question that may keep coming up.

I also have a section for special issues I may be dealing with from time to time, such as forgiveness or negative thinking. And, perhaps most importantly, I make room to record unusual experiences and perceptions that come from my meditations and from quiet times of doing nothing.

Even though we may have greatly simplified our lives and reduced much of the outside stimuli that assault us on a daily basis, it's amazing how quickly we can forget important insights that can help us in our growth. So not only does a journal serve as a device for working on solutions to problems as they arise, but it also serves as a reliable memory.

I'm careful not to become a slave to a journal, however, and I don't feel I have to use it every single day. It's simply there as an ally when I need it.

If you think a journal would be helpful to you on your odyssey, come up with a format that works for you.

I use a six-by-nine-inch spiral-bound notebook and tabulate it for dreams, runes, or whatever, depending on my needs. I find this size is easy to keep on a bookshelf with other books, and is a convenient size to travel with. It is also less forbidding than a larger notebook, and therefore easier to dispose of when it has served its purpose. Thus, it doesn't ultimately become one more thing to clutter up my life.

32. Ask for help if you need it

I GREW UP on the plains of Kansas and was imbued from an early age with a strong belief in rugged individualism and going it alone in the true spirit of the pioneer.

When I found myself in the fiasco that was my first marriage (#81), it never occurred to me to ask anyone for help. I figured I'd gotten myself into this mess and somehow I'd get myself out. Eventually, I did. But if I'd known then what I know now about asking for help, I'd have gotten out a lot sooner, and with a lot less trauma. In fact, I'd never have gotten into it in the first place!

My friend Judy grew up with what those of us who know and love her refer to as a strong sense of entitlement. Her childhood training was just the opposite of mine. She has no hesitation about asking anyone anywhere for help. And the absolutely amazing thing to me is that she always gets whatever help she needs.

I've picked up some valuable lessons watching her over the years. First of all, I've learned that it's okay to need help; it's nothing to be ashamed of. Secondly, I've learned that most people are willing to help someone who simply asks for it.

In addition, I've learned to be careful whom I ask for help. There's no point in going to an auto mechanic if you're having a coronary.

Also, I've learned to distinguish between an everyday, garden-variety upset that a friend or a support group could help with and major distress that requires a professional (#47).

I also make a point of avoiding the person who insists on helping whether I need it or not. I used to be that type before I simplified my life, so I'm familiar with that energy!

If, like me, you're one of those who's never been comfortable asking for help, maybe it's time to rethink your attachment to the pioneer spirit. We're all human, and we all need a little assistance from time to time.

Developing the ability to ask for help when you need it will often provide clarity to your life, and enable you to move through life's lessons much more quickly.

33. Ask for help from the universe

AS LONG AS you're asking for help, you might as well ask for help from the universe. You never know what might happen.

A while back I found myself in a particularly confusing and distressful situation. I'd had a counseling session or two for this particular issue. I'd discussed it with friends and family. But I was at an impasse. I simply couldn't seem to get beyond it.

I was driving to an appointment one morning when the seeming enormity of this problem overwhelmed me. I pulled to the side of the road, stopped the car, and turned off the engine. I threw up my hands and yelled to whoever was "out there" that might be paying attention, "Okay! I give up! I need some clarity and some relief on this one. Help!"

I pounded the steering wheel furiously several times for emphasis. I sat there silently for a few moments, feeling completely drained. Eventually, I started up the car and went to my meeting.

A short time later I noticed I was feeling a tremendous sense of release from this problem. As the day wore on, I began to get an understanding about it that I simply hadn't been able to come to before. I couldn't even quite put it into words; I just knew that I had passed through the worst of it, and that I'd soon be able to put it behind me.

Obviously, this is nothing new. We've all had similar experiences. Some might call this prayer and say God was listening. Others would call it a higher power. Still others would say it was my higher self responding to my desperation. I like to think of it as the power of the universe.

Call it what you will, there is an energy available to us. All we have to do is ask for it. And we don't have to wait until things get desperate. We can use it as a regular part of our everyday lives, for guidance, for inspiration, for getting in touch with our true selves.

I've learned that the more I call upon this help, the more it's available to me. I have a sense that, as I continue to utilize it in my life, my comprehension of it will expand as well. Enlarging our concept of the power that's available to us, and using it regularly in our daily lives, can only enhance our inner growth.

34. Figure out what others have to teach you

EVERY NOW AND then, you'll find yourself con-nected with someone who just drives you up the wall. There may be any number of reasons you can't get away from this person for the time being.

Or maybe you've gotten away, but you run into them from time to time, and they zap your energy. Soon you find yourself spending inordinate amounts of time grumbling to yourself about all the things they do that make you nuts.

Or maybe you don't see them at all anymore, but you still spend a lot of time grousing about the way they are, or fuming over something you think they did to you in the past. Usually, this is someone you once had a close relationship with.

When this kind of thing happens, you can be certain this person is in your life or in your mind for a reason: there is something you need to learn from them before you can put the relationship to rest.

For starters, sit down and spend some time *thinking* about what it is this person does that gets on your nerves. Make a list of the qualities or habits or behavior patterns that bother you. Then look objectively at your own personality. Maybe you have some of these same qualities, and you want, at some level, to get rid of them.

Or maybe you already have made changes in these areas, and it's disturbing to you to think that you were once like that. Often, once you get clear exactly what it is that bothers you, it's easier to let go of it.

Possibly this person actually did hurt you, perhaps intentionally. If you just can't seem to find it in your heart to forgive them yet (#70), force yourself to sit down again and make a list of all the people *you* may have harmed, either accidentally or on purpose.

It's even possible you've hurt *this* person in some way. Look at that same dark space you were coming from when those things happened and realize that, though you have moved away from that place, the person you're dealing with may still be operating in the dark.

Perhaps what this person has to teach you is how far you've come, and that in order to move on you've got to develop some compassion, for them and for yourself. When it comes right down to it, it would appear we're all in this together.

At some intuitive level we all know why we're in the situations we're in. The objective is to reach a point where we can understand what those reasons are, make whatever changes we need to make, and then move on.

35. Use the events of the day to bring you back

ONE OF THE benefits that comes from slowing down our lives is the ability to get back in touch with who we really are and what we're doing here. It's tremendously liberating to make that connection, but often, because of the demands of our work schedule and the complexities of family and social obligations, we keep forgetting.

Get into the habit of using the events of your day to remind yourself of the inner realizations you are starting to get a sense of during your quiet times, and to remind yourself to connect with your soul. You can use any circumstance or happening of the day to bring yourself back to the inner you.

When you wake up in the morning, remember. When you brush your teeth, remember. When the water boils for tea, remember.

When the phone rings, remember. When you are stopped at a stoplight, remember. When you sit down to a meal, remember.

When you get upset, remember. When you have a headache, remember. When the kids are cranky, remember.

When you get into bed at night, remember. When you fall asleep, remember.

36. Find a teacher

THERE ARE THOSE who say that when you're ready to step onto your spiritual path, a teacher will appear to show you the way. This may be true, but it hasn't been my experience yet.

But even though I haven't found that special relationship, I've found that the search for it is part of the journey, and it can be a great adventure.

If you're thinking you might like to find some guidance as you go along, one way is through books.

One book in particular that I found very helpful in outlining the plethora of teachings available today is *The Spiritual Seeker's Guide,* by Steven S. Sadleir. It's an excellent reference for the major spiritual paths, metaphysical initiations, teachers, masters, and movements of the world. It describes not only the teachings and the teachers and tells you where to get more information, but it places each in a historical context, going back to 8000 B.C.

What a review like this provides, in addition to practical

information regarding areas you might want to explore—or avoid—is the realization that all true spiritual teachings attempt to lead ultimately to the same thing: an understanding of the mysteries of the universe and the role we each play in it.

Obviously some teachings do it better than others. And some have gotten corrupted along the way. It also becomes clear that no path is the best path, or the only path, and that there is something for everyone.

Needless to say, a book of this type has its limitations: it can't include everything. But it can give you a start. Then you'll find one thing leads to another. You meet people in one place who can lead you to other people and other teachings, which then can lead you to where you really want to go.

Or you can just listen (#92). This is harder for the more impatient among us, but ultimately it's what we all have to do anyway. Our intuitive guide, if we can simply sit still long enough to hear it, will always lead us in the right direction.

Once you've begun the inner search, your teachers may change fairly rapidly as you go along, or at least your understanding of them will. I've also learned that being too attached to a teacher can potentially hinder your process. The right teachers can provide many valuable teachings, but they can't live your life for you. Ultimately, we all have to be responsible for our own growth.

37. But don't get too attached

I HAD THE good fortune when I started the first leg of my inner journey years ago to be associated with several loving and helpful mentors who gave me a different perspective of the spiritual path than the one I'd acquired from the religion of my childhood.

They didn't have all the answers, but they provided what I needed at that time in my life. They broadened my horizons, then sent me on my way. In the long run, that may be the most we can expect from a good teacher.

In the process of looking for a teacher, I also did a lot of exploration on my own. If I heard about a mind-expanding technique or a guru who sounded interesting, I would check it out. Some were legitimate, others not. All were instructive. And, in one way or another, they were all part of the journey.

At one point in my youth I heard about a young "master" who was giving "knowledge" to anyone who wanted it badly enough to pin him down for it. As it happened, he had made a trip from India and was temporarily based in Houston.

On a whim I took a week of unpaid vacation, got into a van with half a dozen other seekers, and headed south. The Astrodome was filled with all manner of people looking for the answer. Many of them didn't know what the question was.

But after waiting days and days, those of us who wanted it got knowledge, an ancient meditative technique that was revealed to us in small dark rooms by thin guys wearing white robes. It was supposed to help us achieve cosmic consciousness. I didn't know what that was, but I figured since they were passing it out, I'd take some.

Several months later word spread that one of the more comely devotees had been impregnated by the pudgy little guru. Eventually this charlatan was sent back to India.

I left the fold at that point, and it took me years to admit publicly that I'd been so naive as to fall for that impostor. But advancing years have led me to see the benefits of that experience. After all, I got to go to Houston, where I'd never been before, and I picked up an interesting and effective meditative technique that I used on and off over the years.

I didn't achieve cosmic consciousness as promised but,

all things considered, it was not a bad teaching. And, contrary to what I wanted to believe then, I've since learned that enlightenment rarely happens overnight—and probably only very rarely in the Houston Astrodome.

The point is, if you stumble in your search for enlightenment, don't be afraid to pick yourself up, dust yourself off, and start all over again. And just keep listening. If I'd been listening back then, I'd never have gotten into the van.

38. Ignore the skeptics

A S YOU START to go within and begin to make some changes in the way you look at life and how you spend your time, you may begin to hear teasing remarks from family and friends who haven't yet begun to explore the inner levels. For the most part, they mean no harm. Simply smile, and ignore them.

Don't let this be a difficult thing for you. *You* know the changes that are taking place in your own mind and heart and soul. And even though you may not have entirely figured out the mysteries of the universe, don't let others who don't have a clue distract you. The only thing you have to answer to is your own growth.

If you find yourself in situations where people are needling you a bit, there are a number of things you can do.

If possible, avoid them. A good friend of mine used to spend time with a couple she knew. The husband could seldom pass up the opportunity to poke fun at anyone who ventured to explore anything he considered off the beaten path.

Even though my friend recognized that his comments were without malice, his closed-mindedness became limiting for her. She gradually stopped seeing them.

If that's not feasible, keep your sense of humor. Make a lighthearted comment to diffuse any heavy energy. You can also ignore them, or just listen, and figure out what these people have to teach you.

Above all, keep your own counsel (#72), and remember there may have been a time in the not too distant past when you were a skeptic, too.

39. Establish a routine

I'VE FOUND IT most helpful to have a regular routine for my inner activities.

Now that I've simplified my life, I find it easy to get up at the crack of dawn, or even earlier. In that quiet time I can do yoga and stretching, write in my journal, do some deep breathing, work on affirmations and visualizations, meditate, or have some quiet time to just sit and think.

Then I usually take a brisk walk with Gibbs and our little dog, Piper, before I come back to have breakfast and begin my workday.

Depending on the type of work I'm doing, I've found it beneficial to take a brief meditative break around noon to clear my head, and maybe do some more stretching and deep breathing.

I also try to make a point of reconnecting with nature in the middle of the day, either by having lunch outdoors on a park bench, or by taking a brief stroll after I eat.

I used to have another meditation just before bedtime,

but found I'd often sleep right through it. I've discovered it is much more effective to meditate at the end of my workday, just before dinner. In addition to whatever happens at an inner level, it also clears my head and my psyche for a relaxing evening. Then I take a few minutes before I go to bed to review my day (#41).

I keep this agenda flexible, and it changes from time to time as my patterns change. But having a routine makes it easier to keep in touch with my inner work, and I find I can go with the flow of the schedule. At the end of the workday, for example, my mind and my body are accustomed to a meditation, and I can just ease into it gently with no struggle.

As you expand your awareness and the level of the inner simplicity you want to achieve, think about arranging a convenient routine to make it easier for your inner efforts to fall into place.

40. Break your routine once in a while

EVEN THOUGH IT'S helpful to have a daily routine, getting too attached to it can limit your growth. I've found it tremendously beneficial to completely break the pattern from time to time.

Every now and then, I stop meditating for a couple of days, possibly even a week. I also stop or cut back on the other inner practices I've been developing.

Partly what breaking the routine does is create some confusion and some insecurity in our psyche. This is beneficial because it forces us to *think* about what we're doing. It gives us a chance to take a close look at whether these activities are contributing to our inner growth, or if they're just something else we feel we *have* to do.

Rituals and habits are important, but if we forget why we're doing them, or if they've lost meaning because at some level we've moved beyond them, then they become one more meaningless ceremony that isn't adding anything positive to our lives.

Breaking the routine also keeps us open to trying new things. What works for you today may not necessarily work for you next month, or next year.

Like all growth, inner growth is a process. Once we've learned to crawl, then we can learn to walk, and then we can learn to run. Breaking the routine from time to time insures that we won't get stuck in the crawling. Also, it helps to remind us that the things we do to make up the routine are simply tools for our inner expansion. Don't mistake the tools for the growth.

41. Review your day

ANOTHER PRACTICE THAT might be help-
ful in your inner search is taking a few minutes each
evening just before bedtime to review your day.

Go to your sanctuary (#27), and start by sitting quietly
for a few moments to let the vibes from the day settle down.
Take a couple of long, slow, deep breaths, and consciously
relax your body. Have the *intention* of getting rid of any worries or concerns. If you're tuned in, you can actually *feel* any
negative energy slowly dissipate.

Then do a quick review of your day, and take particular
notice of any issue you may want to deal with. Do what you
can to to bring a level of understanding to this, either by simply thinking it through or perhaps by working at the alpha
level (#30). Then release it to the universe. Sometimes I've
found just letting go of a dilemma brings a clarity that will
help me address it later from a more enlightened point of
view.

You can sit there for a few blissful moments and be

grateful for your day, and perhaps jot some notes in your journal. You can contemplate, do some deep breathing, or prepare for your dream explorations. If you're developing any new practices you want to incorporate into your life—or getting rid of any bad habits—have your calendar and box of stars handy so you can chart your progress (#61).

Basically, these few minutes at the end of the day give you a chance to slow down, unwind, enjoy the silence, and tap into any messages from the universe that might assist you as you go along. Not only will it help you stay on course for the things you want to accomplish at an inner level, but clearing away any mental, emotional, or psychic clutter will make it easier for you to get a good night's sleep.

When you spend time reviewing your life on a daily basis, you'll see that each day presents an opportunity to live your life exactly the way you want to. Imagine yourself moving into the best you can be, and then living each subsequent day from that perspective. With time, you'll get better and better at doing this.

42. Smile a lot

IF YOU'VE STARTED to slow down and simplify your life, if you're spending time in nature and have surrounded yourself with beauty, if you've latched on to synchronicity and tuned into your creativity, and if you've learned to enjoy each moment, you're probably already smiling a lot.

In fact, you may find yourself absolutely grinning from time to time for no apparent reason.

And, once you start doing some of the harder stuff in the next couple of chapters, you may well find yourself positively ecstatic.

Once you free yourself from anger (#66), or worry (#64), or negative thinking (#63), your life will be so much simpler.

Once you learn to detach (#49), overcome your fears (#50), and learn to say no (#54), your load will be so much lighter. Your heart and mind and soul will be free. Things will somehow start to make sense. It'll happen spontaneously. There's nothing to be done about it. Don't question it. Don't doubt it. Don't apologize for it. Don't gloat. It just happens. Enjoy it. And keep on smiling.

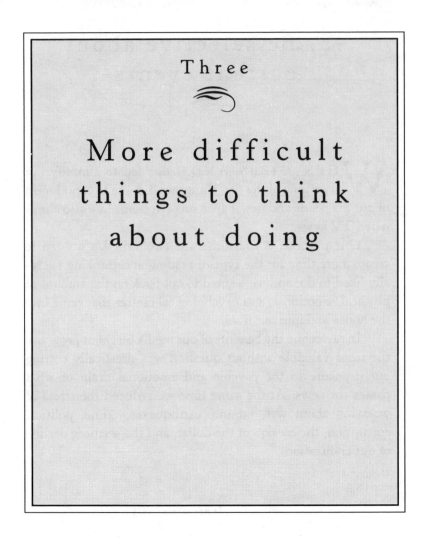

Three

More difficult
things to think
about doing

43. Be selective about current events

WHEN GIBBS AND I decided to simplify our lives, one of the first things we did was to cancel most of our magazine and newspaper subscriptions. We also eliminated TV news.

Our purpose at that time was twofold: We wanted to create more time for the type of reading and thinking we really liked to do, and we wanted to cut back on the amount of physical, emotional, and psychological clutter that came into the house and into our lives.

In reviewing the benefits of our media blackout program, the most valuable without question was drastically cutting our exposure to the psychic and emotional drain of what passes for news. At the same time we reduced the stress of worrying about war, famine, earthquakes, crime, political corruption, the erosion of the dollar, and the seeming decline of our civilization.

As you start to go within, you might want to think about cutting back on the amount of time you spend keeping up with current events. Few things can disrupt your inner tranquility faster than a jolt of bad news, especially when you're just starting out on your journey. The worst part is that until we're tuned in to our inner selves, we're often not even aware of the adverse impact tuning in to the apparent problems of the world can have on us.

After years of allowing myself to manipulated by the negativity of newsmongers, I found it was tremendously empowering to be able to pull the plug and to create the space for positive messages instead.

There'll always be people and organizations hawking bad news. And there'll always be people who are addicted to it, even though they may not be aware of it. But if you're embarking on a spiritual journey, it's very likely that your desire for real growth will become greater than your need to be constantly in the know.

At the very least, you might want to be selective about the type and the amount of news you allow yourself to be confronted with. Eliminating even some of the psychic clutter of bad news will greatly facilitate your inner quest.

44. Reduce your need to be in the know

FOR YEARS MY friend Sue has limited her exposure to the daily news. Frequently people ask her how she responds when someone asks her what she thinks about the latest current event.

She tells them she tries not to think about current events. It has taken her many years to get to the point where she could admit publicly that the latest news is simply not a major interest of hers. She's also learned not to let other people make her feel guilty because *they* choose to spend their time tracking some hot news story.

If what's happening in the news is your passion, then you'll obviously want to stay informed. But if you're keeping up with the news just so you can appear to be in the know when someone who's doing the same thing asks you about it, perhaps you need to do a priority check (#13). Do you really want to spend your time and energy immersing yourself in bad news so you can seem knowledgeable to someone you probably don't even care about?

If you do want to keep in touch with what's happening in the world, it's not necessary to spend hours with the newspaper or in front of the television to do so. Gibbs is a travel writer, and we frequently find ourselves in remote parts of the world for extended periods of time without any connection to the outside world. We've found spending a few minutes perusing a news magazine often provides more information than we want about what has happened in the world in our absence.

Rather than spending hours with a newspaper, you can keep up with world events by scanning the headlines. If you come across a subject that interests you, you can easily explore it further. Often, news reports are packed with misinformation or noninformation anyway, so while we think we might be learning something by spending time reading or watching the news, often we're simply absorbing empty filler.

It's a matter of how you want to spend your time. Once you've begun to explore new possibilities on the inner levels, there's a good chance you'll find these much more satisfying and productive than keeping up with what passes for news.

45. Rethink the beliefs of your childhood

THE NUMBER OF people who have abandoned the religion of their childhood is legion. Many people are able to leave and never look back. Others leave, but are often consumed with guilt for doing so.

Some people spend years feeling angry and bitter about the restrictive, small-minded thinking they've spent their lives overcoming. And many continue to feel adversely affected—sometimes unconsciously—by the dogma and the belief systems that permeated their minds as children.

There are also those who never had a childhood religion to leave behind, and who still basically believe in nothing. And there are those who have allowed the predominant conclusion of pseudoscience—which says if we can't prove it, it doesn't exist—to rule their thinking.

If you're beginning to take a look at your life, this might be a good time to examine any feelings you may have about the teachings of your childhood that could be holding you back from questions you really want to explore.

All the great philosophers and thinkers of the world, from Plato to Monty Python, have wondered about the meaning of life. If nothing else, you'll be in good company.

As you start to slow down and enjoy the silence and the solitude, as you learn to listen and begin to trust your intuition, as you start to make the changes in your lifestyle and habit patterns that will enable you to connect with your own truth, you'll begin to experience a new way of looking at life and the world and your place in it.

The answers to the age-old questions may not come overnight. In fact, you may have to spend some time in the condition of not knowing. This can be unsettling if you've spent years thinking you knew the answers, or believing there were no questions.

But if you keep at it, the time will come when you'll form your own answers to the questions thinking people have asked from the beginning of time. And these answers will be based not on faith, not on dogma, but on a deep understanding of your own experience.

46. Rethink your current beliefs

WHILE YOU'RE RETHINKING the beliefs of your childhood, don't forget to examine your current beliefs, the ones you may have acquired after you let go of the beliefs of your childhood, the ones you moved into at the time of your midlife crisis, or even the ones you settled into last year, or possibly last week.

It'll be helpful to stay open to new interpretations of the world and how it might work. Often we get stuck in our current thinking because, like an old shoe, it's so comfortable. Move out of your comfort zone from time to time, and keep an open mind.

47. Get some counseling

I T'S FORTUNATE IN many ways that we're living in the age of the dysfunctional family. Even as recently as a few years ago, you were considered an anomaly if you sought professional counseling. Now, if you haven't been in therapy, people assume you're in denial. Take advantage of the times. If you have a problem that neither you, your friends, nor your support group can solve, don't waste another moment. Seek professional help.

Be prepared for the possibility that the first person you see won't have all the answers for you. When I got into counseling several years ago, I made a couple of false starts with inadequate or inappropriate though well-intentioned therapists. I was lucky: I found the right person on the third try. Don't hesitate to look around until you find a therapist you're compatible with. You can't get to the core issues without a basis of trust.

Compatibility isn't the only consideration. You also need someone who's competent and well trained. If you're having trouble finding the right therapist, ask your friends and associates if they know from their own experience who is good. Interview several before you make a decision. Trust your intuition as to which one will work best for you.

Also, don't be put off by the therapy jokes that say you'll have to spend the rest of your life on the couch. If you've found a competent therapist, you should be able to get to the heart of your issues in a couple of sessions.

If you don't get an "ah-ha!" or two fairly early on, think seriously about trying someone else. Once you have a clear understanding of the issues you have to deal with, then the real work begins, and it's not unreasonable to expect to work closely with a good therapist for six months to a year.

Most of us have some kinks that can be straightened out more speedily with professional help than if we attempt our own therapy. Though it may be frightening at first, working with someone who is professionally trained to deal with our wounds and defenses is an effective way to eliminate outmoded patterns that no longer work.

Therapy is one of the many tools we have available today to speed us on our way to understanding ourselves. If you feel you need therapy, don't put it off any longer. It can go a long way toward helping to free you up for the inner business you came here to complete.

48. But don't get stuck in therapy

W E'VE MADE INCREDIBLE progress in the fields of psychology and psychotherapy in the last twenty-five years. We've acquired new and valuable insights about the roles our addictions, our families, and our childhood histories have played in our lives and in our ultimate success and happiness.

In addition to competent therapists, there are recovery and twelve-step programs for every type of physical, psychological, and emotional problem imaginable.

These programs, along with many other personal therapies, have provided tremendous help and understanding for people who, in previous generations, simply had no answers and had to live out their lives in quiet suffering.

If you find that psychotherapy brings you to a new level of comprehension about an issue that may have been troubling you, take from it whatever works for you. Incorporate it into your life, and even revel in it for a time, if that seems appropriate.

Then move on.

The urge is strong to hang on for dear life to therapeutic observations that bring relief to our emotional and psychic wounds. Sometimes the relief is so great the tendency is to hang out in recovery much longer than necessary.

Try not to get stuck in therapy. Doing so can make it harder to move on to the position we all have to come to eventually, that of being responsible for our own lives.

49. Practice detaching

WHEN YOU FIND yourself in situations where your blood is boiling or your stomach is churning, try to get into the habit of stepping outside yourself and becoming the observer.

This is easier to do in the heat of the moment if you've practiced it before the battle gets started.

Whenever you find yourself going through a particularly difficult time, make a point of taking five or ten minutes at the end of the day to practice detaching.

Perhaps you've had an argument with a coworker, or a disagreement with your spouse. As soon as you have the opportunity, sit quietly and do some work at the alpha level (#30).

Imagine being back in that scene. See in your mind's eye the *inner you* stepping away from the fracas and simply observing what's going on. Run through the entire argument in your mind with the inner you not being part of it, simply watching from the sidelines.

If you do this consistently, not only will you find that it relieves some of the tension of the current problem you're dealing with, but it will become an automatic response you can fall into when you find yourself in the fray again.

Detaching releases the tension, diffuses the negative energy, and helps you to see the insignificance of this event in the whole scheme of things. It also gives you a chance to see what lessons you might need to learn from this encounter.

50. Do the things you fear

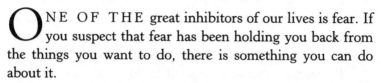

ONE OF THE great inhibitors of our lives is fear. If you suspect that fear has been holding you back from the things you want to do, there is something you can do about it.

Set aside a couple of hours in the next few days, or take some time right now, to make a list of all the things you would like to do but haven't done because you were afraid to. Be honest, and really think about this. No one else ever has to see this list but you.

What would your life be like if you left the town you grew up in to seek your fortune out in the real world, instead of staying home where everything is safe, cozy, and guaranteed? What would your life be like if you gave up the company job, and started your own business as you've always wanted to do?

What would your life be like if you quit the job you can't stand and went back to school to get trained in a field you really love? What would your life be like if you got out of a relationship that wasn't working, and created the space for one that would work for you?

You may be starting to realize that the things you *want* to do are the things you *should* be doing, even if the thought of doing them may be terrifying for you. They are things you came here to do and to experience and to be. Not doing them is holding you back from being the totally full and realized person you can be.

If you can't energize yourself to do the things you fear, there are many seminars you can take and retreats you can attend that will provide you with an opportunity to do some seemingly terrifying feats—like walking across a bed of burning coals, or climbing to the top of a telephone pole and jumping off—that serve as metaphors for the real-life fears we all have to face.

Few things will liberate you faster and move you more quickly along your inner path than doing the things you fear.

51. Share your fears
with someone else

I SAID IN #50 that no one ever has to see the list of things you're afraid of, but in fact, sharing your list with others can be tremendously liberating.

For years my life was ruled by two major fears: the fear of public speaking, and the fear of spiders. I sometimes shudder to think of all the things I didn't do in my life because of these fears. I also shudder to think of all the things I did to keep from having to *admit* to anyone that I had these fears.

Several years ago I found myself in the position of having to confront my fear of public speaking. The publisher of my first book notified me that they were arranging an extensive media tour. I would be appearing before millions of people on national television and radio shows to promote the book. Yiiiiiikes!

I realized that I'd have to do one of two things: either *admit* I had a fear of public speaking (this was unthinkable) or confront my fear and *do the tour* (this was inconceivable). As it turned out, I did both.

Fortunately, at the time I belonged to a tremendously empowering support group (#23). Because I had no choice, I admitted my fears to the group, and asked for help (#32). I didn't realize it at the time, but my battle was half over. Admitting the fear to these allies made it possible for me to start doing the things I had to do to overcome it.

With the help of my group, I was coached and trained and rehearsed. I traveled up and down the coast and spoke to every gathering that would hold still long enough.

By the time the tour came, I was ready. I did the tour, and thoroughly enjoyed the entire process. The combination of overcoming my fear and doing the tour was one of the most incredible experiences of my life. It was a major gift from the universe.

And a funny thing happened on the way to the tour: I discovered that, in the process, I'd also overcome my fear of spiders. I urge you to get out your list of fears and start passing it around. Who knows what might happen.

52. Practice dying

YEARS AGO A yoga teacher I studied with guided us through a meditation in which we confronted our own death. Coming, as many of us have, from a culture in which death was never discussed, much less thought about, I found this somewhat startling at first. But after I'd gone through the exercise a number of times, I began to appreciate the benefits it offered. I started to see death as simply a natural process, and nothing to be afraid of.

Several years later I found myself in the middle of a hurricane with six other people in a very small boat on a very large ocean. I lived for forty-eight hours in the certain belief that we wouldn't survive. When I thought about it later, I was amazed at how calm I felt. It seemed as though I'd done this many times before—which of course I had, through the practice of the dying meditation.

Many cultures throughout history have practiced dying as a ritual. It is a way to confront the fear of death in order to loosen its hold on us. Once you get into it, it can be quite liberating.

So practice dying. Do this as a meditation, and as an exercise in personal growth.

Set aside some time in the next week to imagine your own death. Lie down. Close your eyes. Imagine that you are dying. Where are your friends and family? What do you feel? What are they feeling? Is there anyone you have unfinished business with whom you need to talk to? What would you say to the people you will leave behind?

Then imagine that you are dead. Gone. The End.

This can be terrifying. Even if you envision that you're surrounded by people you love and who love you, there comes a point when you have to take that last step alone. Even though it's only an exercise, go with it. *Experience* that terror. It'll free you.

After you've gone through your first imaginary encounter with your own death, spend some time thinking about other ways you might die: alone in your car on a deserted stretch of highway, or in an airplane crash with hundreds of other people. Run through all kinds of possibilities.

Engaging in the practice of dying, if done with sincerity and as an inquiry into the phenomenon of death, will liberate

you from any fear of death you might have, and free you from
many other fears as well.

Just think how you could live your life with full abandon
if your fear of death were no longer there to hold you back.

53. Release your attachment to possessions

ONE NIGHT, WHILE we were still living in the big house, a huge firestorm came through our area, and we had to evacuate.

Just before we left the house, we looked around and realized how much of the stuff we'd accumulated we could easily get along without.

That's not to say it wouldn't be a hassle if all our possessions got destroyed, and it's not to say that we wouldn't miss some of them. But we'd gotten to a point where we could enjoy our stuff while we had it, and at the same time we wouldn't be devastated if we lost it. That was a big step toward liberation for us.

As it happened, our house didn't burn down. But we saw the evacuation as a good exercise to go through, not only for the uncluttering we ultimately did to simplify our lives, but for releasing our attachment to possessions and achieving a level of inner contentment.

Look around your house and imagine you have thirty minutes to evacuate, and the only things you can take with you are what you can fit in the back of your car. What would you take? If you had to start all over again, how would you do it differently?

We don't have to wait for nature to intervene. We can take responsibility for our lives and begin right now, today, to get rid of the things, and our attachments to the things that get in the way of our inner peace.

When you get right down to it, it's surprising how little we need to be happy.

54. Just say no

WHEN I WAS a young girl growing up in Kansas, I would accept invitations to my friends' birthday parties. But when the day of the party arrived, I invariably didn't want to go. My mother would always say to me, "Oh, Elaine, just go. You know you always have a good time." So I would go, and mother was right: I always had a good time.

It took me *years* to figure out that I always had a good time because I'm the type of person who wouldn't spend four or five hours somewhere having a *bad* time. No doubt you're that type of person, too.

When your friend Jack catches you off guard and invites you to his potluck dinner on Saturday night, you agree to go because you didn't have anything *specific* planned *and* you didn't have an excuse ready. So you end up going.

And often you have a good time. But that doesn't necessarily mean that you wouldn't *rather* have been doing something else, like sitting at home contemplating the meaning of life, or just relaxing and doing nothing.

When Gibbs and I started to simplify our lives we took a look at all the things we did either because we said we'd do them—like going to Jack's potluck—or because we felt we *should* do them—like heading up the fund-raising committee for a group we belonged to—and we stopped doing them. It took us a while, but we finally learned to *just say no.*

When I suggested this to my friend, Peter, he said, "But if I start saying no to people, they'll stop asking me to join them."

When I pointed out that these were people he didn't want to go out with anyway, he said, "Yes, but I want them to *ask* me."

Obviously, you've got to reach the point where your desire to not go is stronger than your wish to be included.

As you begin to listen to your inner voice, you'll start to get a feel for the situations that keep you from being in touch with what you really want to do and who you really want to be. Then you can begin gracefully to avoid them.

You reach a point where you have to be firm, and simply say no those distractions. Your social life may go down the tubes, but this may be just what you need so you can work on your inner growth and create the time and the energy to do the things you really want to do.

55. Examine the costs of not saying no

FOR YEARS I deluded myself into believing things like Jack's potluck involved just a few hours on Saturday night, so it was no big deal. But if you really don't want to do it, it *can* be a big deal.

And it's not just the four or five hours you spend at Jack's that get lost by doing things you don't want to do; it's all the time *leading up* to it, and often the time and energy you spend *recovering* from it as well.

Let's say you've gotten your week simplified to a point where you can spend Saturday and Sunday simply having a quiet, contemplative time getting in touch with your creativity, and painting.

Saturday comes and you've got your canvas set up, and you start thinking about this potluck you really don't want to go to. Just *thinking* about it is an annoyance and an energy drain. Then you realize you don't have anything on hand for the salad Jack asked you to bring. So at some point you have to stop painting, clean up, and run out to the store to get the salad fixings; then you have to make the salad.

Then you have to decide what to wear.

Then you have to get ready. Then you have to go. You've already spent at least several hours, and you haven't even gotten there.

By the time the evening is over, you've eaten a little too much, and you've had too much to drink. You have some coffee to sober you up for the ride home, and then you don't sleep well Saturday night because of the caffeine.

You wake up Sunday feeling groggy because of the lack of sleep, and you have a headache because you drank too much. You feel lousy all day, and there goes the painting.

You've lost part of the day Saturday, all of Saturday evening, and a good deal of Sunday, because you didn't say no to something you didn't want to do in the first place.

As you begin to work on inner simplicity, you'll start to become aware of the number of things you do that you don't want to do. You'll begin to realize how much that detracts from the time you want to spend on your own growth. You may not be able to stop doing *everything* you don't want to do. But you'll get to the point where the next time Jack calls, you'll just say no.

56. Be honest with people

WHEN JACK CALLS, tell him the truth. Simply say, "You know, Jack, I appreciate your asking, but I really *don't* feel like having dinner out on Saturday night. I've been going out too much lately, and I'd really *rather* stay home and spend time with the kids."

If Jack is your friend, he'll understand, even if he might not be happy about it. If he's not your friend, it doesn't matter. If you have a hard time saying no, however, this will still be difficult for you. Practice. Role play, either on your own, or perhaps with your support group (#23).

Remember, you're taking responsibility for your life now, especially the time you need for your inner life. Take a close look at how much time you could save for yourself next week, if you started this week being honest with people by saying no to the things you don't really want to do.

Obviously, there are some social situations where a little white lie is simpler to deal with, not only for you but for the other party as well. But for family and friends with whom you're closely connected, it'll be much more liberating for both of you if you simply and honestly convey your feelings. How *much* you decide to disclose will depend on the circumstances.

You can apply this same philosophy of honesty to any situation you find yourself in. Own up to how you *really* feel about not doing something. If you express your feelings with sincerity, people will accept them.

57. Choose to ignore an insult

THERE IS A Chinese proverb that says it is better to ignore an insult than to have to respond to one. There is such wisdom here.

Think of the troubles you could avoid and the stress you could eliminate if you made the *decision* to ignore a slight offense or a minor defamation, or an unintentional snub—or even an intentional one. Our reactions to the situations of our life are elective, and *we* get to do the electing.

The next time someone is flip with you, fail to notice it. It's a choice. Or choose to laugh (#59). (But do this later, on your own.)

This is not to say you should become a rug and let everyone walk all over you. But you may well find as you continue along your path that it's much more exhilarating to keep your head clear for contemplating the big picture, and not to sweat the little stuff.

Ignoring an insult is a very effective way to keep from getting bogged down in someone else's negative energy, or even in your own.

58. Be patient

ONE OF THE exciting things about the culture and the times in which we live is that we can do almost anything we want to do. Our advancing technology makes it possible for us to have and do things that previous generations never dreamed of. We've gotten used to the instant gratification of our wants and desires. This makes being patient more challenging than it might be otherwise.

As we begin to go within and start to address the big issues (#73), as we learn to love (#100) and to forgive (#70), as we overcome our fears (#50) and learn to just say no (#54), it becomes easier to create happier, more fulfilling lives.

But there will still be hurdles to overcome. The technology is not yet available that would make it possible for us to conquer our demons overnight. The process of growth in any endeavor can often seem like one step forward and two steps backward.

Sometimes I'm disconcerted when I look at my list of things I've wanted to accomplish. Six months ago I may have checked forgiveness (#70) off my list, only to find now that it's back in my life again as an issue I have to deal with. It seems as though I have to start all over. But as I begin to examine it, I see how much the things I've previously done have helped.

Use your journal as an ongoing means of gauging how far you've come in terms of tackling some of your personal challenges.

Learn to be patient with yourself. Enjoy the process of inner growth for what it is—an ongoing opportunity to become the best we can become at all levels of our life.

Don't push the river. Just let it flow.

59. Laugh a lot

EVERY DAY FOR the next week, spend five or ten minutes laughing, first thing in the morning. Do this in your sanctuary, at your kitchen table, or wherever works for you. This won't be easy. We are not encouraged to laugh a lot in this culture. But if you do it, you'll be amazed at the insight it will give you.

You'll probably have to start by faking it. You may have to fake it all the way through. That's okay. Pretend you're an actor, laughing for a part. It's easier if you stand, or sit on the edge of a chair. After the first few times, your stomach muscles will ache a bit. It's nothing to worry about. Keep at it.

When you're finished laughing, sit quietly and *receive* (#12). Let your body and your psyche and your soul absorb the benefits of this. Then start your day.

It's very powerful to do this with someone else who is amenable, but don't let the absence of an available person keep you from laughing. It's just as effective to do it on your own. Don't start crying during the laughing. The crying comes later (#84).

When the week is up, or possibly even sooner, you'll see that it's possible for you to laugh at *anything;* that laughter is a choice. That's a very powerful tool to have when you're working on some of this harder stuff. It's a powerful tool to have, period.

As you move along in your quest, and as you encounter seemingly difficult situations, don't forget to use this tool. It will change your life.

Also, make a point of spending time with people who make you laugh. Rent funny videos. Read funny books. Laughing is so good for the soul.

Four

The
hard stuff

60. Realize the importance
of self-discipline

T HERE'S NO GETTING around it: many of the
steps we must take to achieve inner simplicity require
self-discipline.

Recently, while trying to eliminate a particularly recalci-
trant habit, I remembered a system I developed when I was
eight years old that, more than anything I've ever done,
helped me build self-discipline. Just for fun, I tried it again to
see if it still worked. It did. So I'm passing the idea on to you
here, for whatever it's worth.

When I was in the third grade I woke up one day and
realized I was the only kid I knew who was still sucking my
thumb. I wanted desperately to stop, but after eight years the
habit was deeply ingrained. Nothing I did seemed to help.

Then I got the bright idea of giving up thumb-sucking
for Advent. So I rounded up a Lahey Mortuary calendar—the
kind with a pretty picture on the top half and the days of the

month in one-inch squares on the bottom half—and hung it on my wall next to my bed where I was forced to look at it every night. And I went out and got a box of stick-on gold stars.

My agreement with myself was that I'd get a gold star for every day I got through without sucking my thumb. By the time Advent was over I'd stopped the habit, and as an added benefit, I'd started building self-discipline.

Many times over the years I called on that same system for developing discipline, both for starting good habits and for getting rid of bad ones. Somewhere along the way I gave up the gold stars, but through the years I've used a one month time-frame to keep track of my progress in whatever discipline I'm trying to establish.

Rewards are also an important factor when you're dealing with habits—though if you're motivated enough, getting rid of the offending habit may be its own reward. Obviously, motivation is the key. The calendar and the stars are simply visual tools to help keep track of your progress, evaluate your success, and spur you on to the end of the month.

You may think gold stars are not sufficient reward for you at this point in your life, though they're probably cheaper and less fattening than one of your addictions. And this whole idea may sound childish and absurd to you, which it is. But it works. I strongly urge you to humor yourself here. Recapture some of your childhood enthusiasm and get excited about gold stars. Besides a couple of dollars for the box of stars, and possibly a bad habit, what have you got to lose?

61. Find a box of stars

S O HERE ARE some specific steps you can take to develop self-discipline:

1. Get your calendar and a box of stars.
2. Decide what discipline you want to work on. Let's say you want to eliminate your habit of worrying.
3. Check your motivation level. If you're not fully committed to breaking this habit, you're wasting your time.
4. Don't tell *anyone* what you're doing, or what the stars mean. This dissipates the energy. But do make a private coded note to yourself in the upper left hand corner of the calendar, so you can look back and evaluate your progress in each habit you've worked on.
5. Keep your calendar where you'll be certain to check it every day.
6. At the end of each day, take a look at your calendar and think about your day. If you were able to nip each worry in the bud as soon as you became aware of it, pull out a gold star and place it in the appropriate date box.

7. Always start on the first of the month and go through to the thirtieth. If by the end of the month you've got stars on each and every box, you're on your way. Studies have shown that it takes twenty-one days to change a habit pattern. If that's true, then three weeks would work as well. But a month is such a convenient block of time. You start on the first of the month, and end on the thirtieth, and there you are.

Also, if it's now the fifteenth of the month, and you've decided to break a bad habit, you still have roughly fifteen days to indulge yourself in the old one— or until you have to start on the new one.

If you don't have a star in *every* box, congratulate yourself for the stars you do have, but realize you'll have to start the process all over again next month until you have an entire month with stars on every day.

If you miss a few days in between, don't make the mistake of thinking, "Oh well, I'll just wait until the first of the next month and start again." No. No. No. That won't work. If you stop to wait for the first of next month after missing a couple of days, you're only kidding yourself. You need to do a motivation check.

Even if, by the end of the month, you don't have stars on every day, you're still working at it. Once you've got stars on *every single day,* then you've broken the back of your habit. (It recently took me three months of constant vigilance to eliminate a bad habit.)

8. Once you've achieved a level of self-discipline in one area, go to the next habit you want to work on. Soon, you'll have established a pattern of self-discipline you can easily apply to *any* area of your life.

62. Harbor no thought that will burn

I'VE ALWAYS THOUGHT of myself as a positive thinker. I grew up believing each of us can, for the most part, do anything we truly want to do. I've made it a practice to avoid people who include "can't" in their vocabulary.

Therefore it came as a great surprise to me to discover, once I had started to do some work on the inner levels, that even though I was a possibility thinker, it didn't necessarily mean I was always a *positive* thinker. In fact, from time to time over the years I'd engaged in less than congenial thinking.

It gradually began to dawn on me that I'd have to do a major overhaul of my thought patterns.

Letting go of negative thinking might seem to be a never-ending battle. Our thoughts define our universe, and if we've spent years operating out of negative thought patterns—sometimes seemingly successfully—there can be a part of us that doesn't want to give it up.

Perhaps you know the type of thinking I'm referring to: the huffing, and puffing, and steaming, and fuming over insignificant inanities that never in a lifetime are worth the emotion spent on them. It's not difficult to figure out the kinds of thoughts that are keeping you from having peace of mind, and from moving on to a higher level of being.

You can glom on to every tool in your arsenal to overcome negative thinking. Use affirmations and visualizations. Connect with nature. Do some deep breathing. Every time you have a negative thought, use it as a *reminder* to get back to positive thinking (#35). Develop self-discipline. Keep your energy up. Chant. Meditate. Use your journal, or your pillows (#66). Or ask for help from the universe (#33).

It may take a major effort, but it will be vital for progress on your inner path to become aware of the self-defeating mental grooves you function in, and to make the decision to change them.

63. Try a modified version
of an ancient technique

I WAS AMUSED recently to hear the story of a sage who grappled centuries ago with the issue of negative thinking. As a young man this fellow realized that, if he allowed them to, his negative thoughts would completely control his life, and he'd never get to heaven. So he decided to do something about them.

He acquired two stacks of pebbles, one dark and one light, which he placed outside his hut. Every time he had a negative thought, he'd take a pebble from the dark stack and place it in a pile. When he had a good thought, he'd take a white pebble and place it in another pile.

In his youth, the dark pile was larger than the white pile. However, as he went on in life, the white pile began to completely overshadow the dark pile. By the time he was ready to depart this world at an advanced age, he had completely conquered his negative thinking. No doubt he went straight to heaven.

My first urge, on hearing this tale, was to call up our local gravel supply company and have them drop off a couple of tons of pebbles. But, on reflection, that seemed impractical. After thinking about it for a while, as an experiment—and because I believe we have to have some fun along the way—I came up with what I think is a suitable, slightly modified alternative: black beans.

Actually, any type of bean would work. Get two cups. Fill one with uncooked beans. Keep both cups on your desk, or wherever you spend the majority of your time. The absolute first moment you see a dark thought lurking around the edges of your mind: bam! you have to make a beeline to the full cup, take out a bean, and place it in the other cup.

At the end of the day, check your cup and do a tally, which you can keep track of on your discipline calendar, or anywhere that's handy. This exercise will give you an incredibly clear picture of the amount and the variety of the less-than-positive thinking you engage in.

Once you're aware of your thought patterns—either negative thinking, worrying, judging, or whatever—you can begin to control them, and replace them with the kind of thinking you'd rather concentrate on. By elevating your thoughts you elevate your consciousness and accelerate your inner growth.

64. Stop Worrying

WORRY, LIKE NEGATIVE thinking, is a habit. And, like negative thinking or any other habit, it can be broken once we become aware of it. But worry is sometimes so subtle and so insidious—and so pervasive in our society—that we can worry for years and not even be aware of it.

I learned this lesson a few years back when I had completed a major promotional project for a company I worked for. After months of long, hard, demanding hours and many sleepless nights when I would lie awake worrying if everything would be all right, the deadline was met and the project was finally completed. It was out of my hands; there was not a single thing more I could possibly do about it.

One night a few weeks later, before I had had a chance to start another project, I realized I was still waking in the middle of the night and lying there worrying—even though there was *nothing* at all to worry about. Perhaps this same thing has happened to you.

As I lay there, I had one of those lightbulb experiences we all have from time to time. I saw in a flash that I'd been moving through life from one worry to the next. I examined each of the circumstances as I could remember them, and it became clear that not only had there never been anything to worry about, but worrying had never served any useful function. It was totally wasted energy that kept me from experiencing the joy of the moment and from getting any real sense of accomplishment from my work.

If you're a worrier, think about using the black bean system (#63), or any other method that works for you, to become aware of of the extent of your habit. Then, if necessary, use the discipline calendar (#61) to eliminate worries from your life.

A worry-free life is incredibly liberating, and it will help you achieve inner peace.

65. Stop judging others

ONE OF THE problems that comes from being raised in a patriotic and chauvinistic culture like ours is that we are bred from birth to believe in our own superiority.

It's not only patriotism that instills this conviction. Our religions, our ethnic backgrounds, our educational and cultural training, and the media advertising we are exposed to all teach us, sometimes inadvertently, that we're supposed to be better than the next guy.

Often, we go through life believing it's natural to look down on someone else because of the way they dress, where they live, the work they do, the amount of money they have in the bank, and whether or not they use deodorant soap.

This pervades every area of our lives. We are bombarded daily with hundreds of judgments, many of which we're not even consciously aware of.

When we start to glimpse the possibility that we're here for reasons other than owning a house on two acres and a four-wheel drive vehicle, we get the opportunity to take a look at our judgments and to see how they get in the way of our inner growth.

Once you start to understand that *you're* here for some other purpose, then you have to make the connection that we're *all* here for some other purpose, even if we don't all realize it, and even if we don't know what that purpose is yet.

At some point we begin to get the picture that we're all in this together, and that we're each doing the best we can with what we've got. It's not our place to judge where someone else is on their path.

The process of learning to suspend our judgment about other people and situations can be a particularly arduous one because we have so much training to overcome. But, as with other habit patterns, overcoming it starts with the awareness of how judgmental we are in every area of our lives.

Once we begin to see how often we subtly dismiss others because they don't live up to our standards, we can slowly start to let go of our judgments and get back to trying to figure out what *we* came here to do. And then get on with it.

66. Get rid of your anger

EVERY MORNING FOR the next week before you start your day, go to your bedroom, close the door, and pile all your pillows in the center at the head of the bed. Kneel on the bed with the pillows in front of you. Bow gently to your inner self and to the universe. Then start beating the living daylights out of the pillows.

Do this as a spiritual exercise. Use either your fists, or another pillow, or a plastic baseball bat. Do it for five to ten minutes, or longer if that feels appropriate.

When the time is up, fall into a heap on the bed and breathe deeply until you catch your breath. When you've come back to your center, get up, kneel on the bed as before, and bow again to yourself and the universe. Then go about your day.

You won't believe the incredible feeling of lightness you'll have after doing this. There are so many messages waiting to come to us, but they can't easily move through the negativity of anger and the bad feelings we frequently carry with us.

Get in touch with how you deal with anger. Do you clam up? Do you harbor burning thoughts? Do you take your anger out on others? Whenever you find yourself reacting in these or any other counterproductive ways of denying anger, go to the pillows and beat the living daylights out of them for at least five minutes, or as long as it takes. Teach your kids to do this, too.

If you have any anger you've been carrying around, or if you even *suspect* that you might, this will be one of the most powerful and liberating things you can do.

You may have to replace your pillows frequently. But that's probably preferable to having to replace your stomach lining, or a heart valve.

67. Ask what's happening

~~~

W HEN YOU FIND yourself embroiled in any kind of less-than-joyous emotion, such as anger, or frustration, or impatience, or worry, or negative thinking, take a moment and simply ask yourself, "What's happening here?" Try to figure out what is taking you away from your center.

When you can say, "Ah, that's anger" or "That's worry," then you know what you're dealing with. You can figure out what you're angry about or worried about, and then work on it. Often, simply identifying what's happening will be enough to relieve your distress.

If you're angry, get to your pillows as soon as possible (#66). Or get some fresh air. Or connect with the sun (#3). Remember to do some deep breathing (#96), which is good for almost anything that ails you.

It's possible that you're simply tired, hungry, or thirsty, and that your body and psyche are responding accordingly. If you don't stop to notice what's happening, it's so easy to end up being tired *and* angry *and* frustrated all at the same time. Then you're completely miserable and you don't know why.

Try living your life in the belief that our *natural* state is pure joy. It's when we're truly happy that we're in touch with our souls. The pain and the suffering we feel through any negative emotion or experience is simply a way to tell us how *not* to live. When we learn to identify what's going on, we can make the changes we need to make to get back into our natural state.

68. Take responsibility for your life

THERE ARE THOSE who say that, metaphysically, we choose all the circumstances of our life—our parents, our health, our physical characteristics, our race, and our cultural and geographical orientation—before we are born, and that we come into this life knowing, at some level, that we have to use those circumstances for our inner growth.

I don't know whether this is true, though I like to believe it is. But I do know that if I see my life as my responsibility, then I can make the changes necessary to create what I want and need to be happy.

If I take the position that someone else—a supreme power or whatever—is in charge and will take care of everything, I could be stuck for ages in circumstances I'm not happy about and feel powerless to change them. I've learned that if there's something in my life that doesn't work, and I'm waiting for someone else to fix it, I'd better not be holding my breath.

Nowhere is this more applicable than in the inner realms. If you're already taking responsibility for the outer areas of your life, it will be easier to make the choices you need to make for your spiritual growth.

69. Accept the things you can't change

TAKING RESPONSIBILITY FOR your life also means accepting the things you can't change.

If you're short and want to be tall, or you're an endomorph and wish you were an ectomorph, if you were born with some impediment or acquired one along the way, or if you find yourself in any particular set of circumstances that are absolute, immutable, and irreversible, then you basically have two options. You can rant and rave and curse and indulge in remorse or guilt or self-pity. Or you can go with the hand you were dealt and play the game the best you can.

You can be open to the *possibility* that those who say we have chosen our circumstances are correct, and then set about figuring out what you can learn from your life by making the most of it.

When you look at the personal limitations someone like Helen Keller had to deal with, and the extent to which she overcame them—not to mention the tremendous contribution she made with her life—you can see that it *is* possible to cooperate with the inescapable.

Going within to find the meaning of our lives does not mean seeking to avoid the challenges our circumstances present. Rather it means finding the grace to learn how to live our lives to the fullest extent possible—whatever that is for us—and, in the acceptance, to move on to the highest level of growth we can.

70. Learn to forgive

WHEN I WAS growing up I had an older brother who beat up on me fairly regularly for the first thirteen years of my life. I got little respite until he left home at eighteen to become a Jesuit priest.

Once he was out of the house, my life settled down to what most people would call normal, and I began to forget about all those early traumas with the monster brother. Today we call it denial, but I went on about my life and created the fantasy that I had had a happy childhood, which, for the most part, I did.

But you can't just stuff those early childhood hurts and expect them to go away. At some time, at some level, you have to deal with them.

Many years later I went into counseling to talk about a business relationship that was troubling me, and ended up talking about my brother.

It took months of therapy and personal reflection to uncover the resentment I'd been carrying around with me all those years. When I finally recognized the extent of the trauma, I was certain I'd never be able to forgive him.

As I began to get in touch with my anger, I began to understand why certain patterns and circumstances had been repeated over and over again throughout my life. And gradually I began to see that holding on to that anger was keeping me from truly moving forward. I realized that if I wanted to get on with it, I'd *have* to forgive my brother.

It took me several more years and many quiet hours of contemplation, but finally I was able to pick up the phone, call him, and have it out with him. I was able, in my heart of hearts, to forgive him for all those years of mistreatment.

Soon after that phone call, I started painting, something I had always wanted to do but had never quite been able to get around to. The correlation was so direct there is no doubt in my mind that forgiveness was a key: one month I forgave my brother; the next month I started to tap into my creative core.

I urge you to stop right now and make a list of any people you might be harboring anger or resentment against. Then start working today on forgiveness. You may not be able to come to a position of forgiveness overnight. And you may not be able to do it alone. There are many seminars, books, and tapes available to help you. If necessary, get some counseling

(#47). Do whatever you need to do to get started learning to forgive.

Keep in mind that you don't have to learn forgiveness for the benefit of the person who may have wronged you, but for the liberation of your own soul.

71. Get out of relationships that don't support you

WE HUMANS, FOR the most part, still maintain our herd instincts. It's comforting to be one of the pack, and to have family, friends, and loved ones near by to help us grow, at least at the start of our journey.

But it sometimes happens that the people we are closest to don't really support us. Look around you, not just at your spouse and the family members you're involved with, but at all the relationships and associations you have in your life. The lack of support can be so subtle. We can hang out for years with someone we love and think of as a friend before we begin to realize that the relationship isn't really helping us and, in fact, has been holding us back.

It's easy to be deceived by the comfort a longtime relationship appears to offer you. There's a certain ease that comes with familiarity and from knowing each other's history, and from the history the two of you have built together, even when it's been tumultuous.

But there comes a time when you have to ask some hard questions: Does that person really love you, or are they hanging on to you because of their own lack or their own needs? They may *say* they love you, but do they make you *feel* loved? Are they really happy with you in your successes, or do they always manage to put you in the wrong? Do they love you enough to let you go on to bigger and better things, even if it means they get left behind?

Nonacceptance and subtle putdowns can be powerful deterrents to your growth. If you're not getting the love and support you need from the relationships in your life, it'll be much harder for you to achieve inner simplicity.

If you're moving on, sometimes there is really no choice but to leave behind those who may not be ready to move on with you.

Often you simply have to retreat with a smile, and gradually but *resolutely* reduce their presence in your life.

Realize that all the family ties and friendships in your life are there for a purpose, but they aren't necessarily meant to last forever. It takes a certain grace to recognize when the time for a disabling relationship is over and, even if the other person doesn't recognize it, to bow out and move on. You'll then have the time and energy to concentrate on loving, supportive relationships.

72. Keep your own counsel

IF YOU'RE JUST starting out on your journey, you'll have to walk a fine line between sharing the joy of your new discoveries with friends and family and being sidetracked by the negative energy of those who don't understand what's happening.

Learn to zip your lip. At the very least forgo the urge to share each new glimpse of your inner world with everyone around you.

Also resist the temptation to have everyone you know hop on your wagon. We each have our own path to follow, and what works for you may not be relevant to the next person. Recognize ahead of time that the inner path can be exciting and very fulfilling, but sometimes lonely.

There's also a difference between getting the help you might need from friends (#32), or a support group (#23), or from counseling (#47), and baring your soul about the progress you are making on your spiritual trek to everyone who comes along.

For those who ask, explain in general terms that you're

doing some soul-searching, and are beginning to look at your life in ways you've never done before. If you're not in friendly territory, there is no benefit to being specific. Whatever you do, don't get defensive. Arguing with someone over the rightness of your path can only lower your energy and set you back. You don't have time for that. *For those who don't ask, say nothing.*

Also, be cautious about getting distracted by the inner search of new people you'll be meeting along the way. What they're doing or the teacher they're following may look interesting, but more often than not their path will not be your path. But it'll be so comforting to find others who are searching too, and who perhaps have found answers to some of your own questions, that the desire will be great to hang out with them perhaps longer than necessary.

Learning not to get sidetracked by the energy of others will be one of your greatest challenges. Learning to keep your own counsel will be your greatest defense.

73. Figure out your big issue

WHEN YOU GET right down to it, we all have at least one major issue—and possibly several minor ones—to work on in our lives. Some of us are better at keeping them under wraps than others, but no matter how hard we may work at denying them, even to ourselves, they're right there just waiting for us to deal with them.

In my experience, it's much easier to establish a level of inner simplicity once we recognize what our big issue is, start to work on it, and eventually, eliminate it completely.

My big issue has been anger. I spent so much time as a child being angry at my brother that it became a comfortable habit.

As I grew older and my circumstances changed, I still continued often to react to situations with anger because I was familiar with it, and knew how to operate out of that stance. Several people had pointed it out to me over the years, but I hadn't understood, mostly because, until I started to simplify my life, I'd never taken the *time* necessary to face the issue and deal with it.

Those who are metaphysically inclined say that the big issues in our lives are what we came here to work on and to experience, and that working on them makes it possible for us to move forward. That may be true. At the very least, learning to deal with what I see as my big issue has been tremendously liberating for me. Being able to move beyond it has created the space for a lot more joy. And it certainly has simplified my life.

If you don't know what your big issue is yet, spend some time figuring it out. If you can't do that on your own, ask those closest to you to help. (Often they're only too glad to do this!) The responses you get may surprise you, and you may not want to believe what you hear. It's possible they could be wrong; only you will know for sure.

You may have to do a lot of inner searching and possibly get some counseling before you can come to terms with it. But if you've got an unresolved major issue that has been running your life, such as being a victim, being in denial, being meek, aggressive, jealous, suspicious, vulnerable, or whatever, don't wait any longer to start to work on it. Doing so will free your heart, your mind, your body, and most importantly, your soul.

74. Get your finances under control

THE PATTERNS OF greed, overconsumption, and instant gratification that were prevalent in the 1980s created a lot of financial havoc that many people are still trying to recover from. The movements toward simplicity and spiritual growth seem to be among the leading trends of the 1990s, but it's difficult to concentrate on inner peace if you can't pay the rent.

Often it's the way we spend indiscriminately and the constant media pressure to buy that drains us emotionally as well as financially. We've been led to believe that whether or not we can afford it, there's no reason not to get it—whatever it is. Often we're impelled by advertising hype to part with our hard-earned dollars in exchange for items we don't even want, that end up cluttering up our lives and getting in the way of our personal growth.

If your financial life is suffering from the expansion of

the past decade, it may be time for you to make some drastic changes in the way you relate to money.

There are many books available today that can help you get back on track financially. One of the best, in my opinion, is *Your Money or Your Life* by Joe Dominguez and Vicki Robin. This book will give you a new way of thinking about the time you spend getting money versus how you spend it.

And of course, living simply, as outlined in my book *Simplify Your Life* will reduce your expenses automatically.

Once you establish financial tranquility in your life, inner tranquility will be a lot easier to come by.

75. Get your body in shape

FOR MOST OF us, inner progress is easier if we maintain an optimum level of health and strength, not only to withstand the rigors of our spiritual disciplines, but also to help ward off the negative patterns we encounter in our everyday lives.

But getting in shape and staying in shape is no easy feat in this day of overeating, overdrinking, excessive dieting, junk food, recreational drugs, mostly useless over-the-counter palliatives, and often dangerous prescription remedies.

So where do you start? Remember moderation in all things, then start with your eating habits. Food really *is* our best medicine. If you don't already know what is the best eating program for your body type, do a little research (see Reading List), and a lot of listening to your body's response. Keep not only your health but your energy level in mind when you eat. One of the most destructive things we do to our bodies is to overeat.

Adopt a healthful exercise program. If you've been running and/or exercising yourself into the ground, think about how little exercise we really need to maintain good health, and at how much damage the excessive exercise regimens of the 1980s actually did to our bodies.

Start a healthful exercise program such as walking, and a limbering program such as yoga or stretching. Studies have shown that it's the loss of elasticity in our muscles and the tightening of our joints that create the immobility of our advancing years. Do whatever you need to do to keep your body supple.

Make sure you're getting an adequate amount of sleep. Again, listen to your body. Arrange your routine so you get the sleep you need. Our bodies and our sleep schedules have often been put on the back burner in recent years, but sleep is an important and completely natural way to restore and maintain good health and high energy.

We know that stress is a major cause of illness in our culture. Make whatever changes are necessary to eliminate the tensions in your life. The classic, proven stress releaser is meditation. Simplifying your life, spending time in solitude, and taking your own private retreats are invaluable stress reducers, too. So are laughter (#59) and joy (#99). Make room for them in your life.

76. Keep your energy up

IN ADDITION TO maintaining good health, inner
simplicity also demands a high level of energy. Low energy
can bring with it a myriad of problems such as frustration,
boredom, inertia, depression, and a sense of overwhelming
futility, any one or all of which can make it impossible to
move forward on your spiritual journey.

Start to become aware of the situations and people that
drain your energy.

Look at noise sources such as radios, stereos, television,
shoot-'em-up movies, traffic, and raucous gatherings. Eliminate these and other disrupting aural intrusions from your
life, and notice how your energy goes up.

Do you sense that certain people leave you feeling listless
and off-balance? On the surface, someone you spend time
with may seem perfectly pleasant, but somehow you always
feel worn out after they've gone, as if they took your energy
with them. As much as possible, avoid them.

Allowing yourself to become tired, overworked, overly

hungry, or overexposed to sun and weather can drain your energy. So can idle gossip, personal confrontations, and so-called news reports.

Sometimes you can find yourself completely deprived of energy for no apparent reason. It's important at those times to examine what you've been doing, talking, or thinking about, or what you've been eating or drinking, so you can eliminate as much as possible not only the obvious energy drains but the subtle ones as well.

While you're becoming aware of what gets you down, keep your eyes and feelings open for the situations and the people and the happenings that raise your energy, lift your spirits, and make you feel terrific. Train yourself to actively avoid the energy drains, and to make a point of including the things that make you feel good.

The more negative energy you can rout out of your life, and the more positive energy you can bring into it, the easier it'll be to connect with your soul.

77. Let go of the addictions that hinder your progress

I HAVE A friend who began meditating several years ago. She immediately felt a connection between how her various addictions affected her level of awareness and, without batting an eye, let go of all the foods, drinks, and ingestible substances she had been overly attached to and that she felt were getting in the way of her inner growth.

She adopted a more or less vegetarian diet: stopped drinking alcohol, coffee, and other caffeinated drinks; eliminated processed foods and sugars from her diet because they brought her energy down. She feels she's made tremendous strides in achieving a level of inner growth she wouldn't have been able to make otherwise.

When I first started working seriously on inner growth, I was more inclined to use St. Augustine's approach: Oh God, please make me a saint, but not yet. There's a possibility I'd be much further along on my path toward inner freedom if I'd been able to give up chocolate mousse five years ago, but the elimination of addictions has been a much more gradual process for me.

Many people find, once they start meditating, contemplating, and going within, that the things they eat and drink affect the quietness of their minds. Often, if we're consuming the wrong stuff, it makes it difficult for us to be in touch with what's going on at the inner levels.

Deciding which of your cravings you want to eliminate and how quickly you want to do it is a personal choice, based on your own intuitive reaction to the things you eat and drink. If you're tuned in, you'll know what makes it harder for you to stay in touch with the inner you.

78. Figure out the right foods for you

SOME YEARS BACK I asked one of the teachers I'd met along the way to give me some advice on food. What I wanted was a computer printout that said now, and for the rest of your life, you can eat this and this and this. And you must avoid this and this and this. It would be so simple. With such a list, I'd never have to be concerned about what to eat, and I could just get on with my spiritual quest.

I was mildly annoyed when he said he couldn't do that. He suggested I learn to listen to how my body responded to what I ate, and figure out for myself the foods that would be best for me.

I was into immediate fixes at the time, so I moved from one supposedly miracle dietary plan to the next. After years of doing this, I've finally come to the conclusion that he was right. We each have different nutritional needs, not only at different times in our lives, but at different times throughout the year. Seldom is there one simple program that will always have all the answers for our particular needs.

If your body is not functioning at its best, if you regularly have headaches, muscle aches, stomach problems, or any number of other health issues, take a look at what you're eating and drinking that might be contributing to your discomfort.

A while back I started eating mostly raw vegetables, thinking it would be better for my health. After a few months I began having digestive problems and then muscle aches that developed into bursitis. I thought at first it was simply advancing years, but when I examined it further, I began to make the connection between my supposedly healthful new diet and the way I felt. I finally figured out that my body wasn't able to assimilate the nutrients from raw foods. I started lightly steaming the veggies and my problems cleared up practically overnight.

Of all the health books I've read over the years, one of the best in my opinion is *Perfect Health* by Deepak Chopra. This book is a very readable introduction to the ancient science of ayurveda. It provides a coherent explanation of various body types and explains why and how our food needs differ from person to person and from season to season. It is an excellent guide for maintaining health and balance in your dietary as well as in your physical and spiritual life.

When it comes to specifics, the best way to figure out what we should be eating is to listen. This takes time and patience, and experimentation. But the more you pay attention to your body's responses, the clearer will be the messages that help you decide what the optimum foods are for you.

79. Eliminate your old patterns

W HEN I FIRST started to simplify my life, I made the decision to reduce the time I spent in my office every day. Eventually I was able to arrange my work schedule so I could quit at five o'clock in the afternoon rather than at seven o'clock in the evening.

So almost immediately I had two extra hours each day, or a total of ten to twelve hours each week, during which I could pursue other interests. At first, this felt quite liberating. I could go for walks in the early evening, or sit quietly and meditate or do nothing, or just relax and watch the sunset.

But after a while, I noticed a strong inclination simply to stay at my desk and continue working until seven, as I'd done for many years.

I couldn't quite figure out what was happening. I'd already decided that I didn't *want* to stay and work; I wanted to play or do other things. But staying in the office was so *easy*. I was comfortable, and I knew what I had to do there. If I quit work early, not only would I have to *come up with something else to do,* but then I'd have to get my head and my mind and my body in gear and *do it.*

It took some serious contemplation of this tendency before I realized that it was my well-established pattern that was keeping me in the office. Working late had become a *habit* and as with all habits, it took some serious desire, discipline, and determination to change it.

Keep this in mind as you are beginning to explore the riches of the inner worlds. Often we allow our good intentions—to do some spiritual reading or take some quiet time to think or learn to simply enjoy the silence—to be overpowered by our outdated habits or by insignificant interruptions. Unless we recognize what's happening and make a concerted effort to establish new patterns, it's easy to stay stuck in the old ones.

Sometimes simply being aware that your old habits are resisting being changed is enough to help you move beyond them, though it may still take some effort. If you need more corrective measures, get out your calendar and your box of stars (#61).

80. Get comfortable
with change

GROWTH BY DEFINITION requires change. And that change, as I discovered when I first tried to rearrange my work schedule, can be unsettling. If you've spent years with certain habits, beliefs, and ways of doing things, inner growth may cause some upheaval in your life. Don't be put off by that. Get comfortable with it. Welcome it. Change offers an exciting, often exhilarating way of getting in touch with your soul.

A few years back, when I was in the process of making some career changes, a counselor I was seeing strongly urged me to take a year off and do nothing. Do nothing for an entire year? That possibility and the changes it would bring about in my life were beyond my imagination. For someone like me who'd been moving so fast for so long, there was at some level the fear that if I stopped I'd keel over, or never be able to get going again.

It took many months and many hours of quiet reflection

before I was able to see the wisdom of that advice. Finally, I took the plunge and arranged my business life so that I could take off for an extended period of time. After spending umpteen years knowing *exactly* what I was going to do each day, to get up in the morning and not have a clue was unsettling to say the least. And for someone like me who is a creature of habit and who loves routine, having each day be totally different from the day before was like hanging from a precipice.

But that year of doing nothing was one of the most enlightening and productive years I've ever spent. Not only did I have the opportunity to do a lot of *soul* work and in many ways revolutionize my belief systems, but I was able to get in touch with my *life* work as well. It kept me living on the edge, and got me comfortable with the prospect of change.

I'm not suggesting that you take a year off, though if your life is feeling out of control, that might a good place to start.

But if you find yourself stuck in outdated habits and ways of operating that no longer serve you, spend some time thinking about how you might do things differently. True inner growth might well require that you experience new thoughts, new feelings, new sensations, new friendships, possibly even a new identity. Allow yourself to be vulnerable, and open yourself to change.

81. Learn to see the problems in your life as gifts

W HEN I WAS twenty-three I married a brilliant physician who, by his own diagnosis, was a manic-depressive paranoid schizophrenic with delusions of grandeur. I spent the next four years in hell. They were without question the most miserable years of my life.

Fortunately, I found the strength necessary to get out of that marriage. And also fortunately, I had a wise friend who pointed out to me at the time what a tremendously valuable lesson those years had been for my personal growth. I learned more about human nature and my own strengths and weaknesses than I could have from any other circumstance I can imagine.

As I look back on that marriage now, painful as it often still is to think about, I see that it was one of the greatest gifts the universe has given me. I'm tremendously grateful for that experience, and the positive contribution it made to my life.

If you still think of the mistakes of your life as disasters, I urge you, for the sake of your inner growth, to change the way you think about them. Sit down sometime in the next few days and list the situations, conditions, circumstances, and happenings that you've always seen as problems or negatives.

Take the first item on your list and look at the *benefits* you got from that situation. Look at the other problems you may have avoided because of it. Think of the ways your life is better because of what you learned.

For example, because my marriage was so disastrous, I got out of it much sooner than I would have otherwise, and was able to move on and create a happy and satisfying life for myself. I know many people who've had less than compatible marriages, but because their choices were only bad and not, like mine, *intolerable*, they stayed many years longer in unsatisfying relationships than they needed to.

Of course, I could wish that I'd married right in the first place, but since I didn't, I had two choices: moan about it for the rest of my life, or learn what I could from it, then move on.

Continue through your life and rethink every circumstance you have previously regarded as negative, and see how each one can be used as a step to your inner growth. Start living your life and rethinking your past as though there are no problems. There are only opportunities for enlightenment.

82. Develop gratitude

NOW THAT YOU'VE taken a look at how mistakes can be positive factors in your life, make a list of all the things you've done right, and all the things (in addition to your mistakes) you have to be grateful for.

Look at your family, your friends, your home, your car, your town, your health, your job—the list is endless. It may not all be perfect at the moment, but what isn't perfect you can change.

If you can't change it, you can get rid of it, or move on. At the very least—or perhaps the very most—you can, through counseling or meditation or introspection or help from a variety of sources, learn to live with it. We all have the opportunity at this time and in this place to make our lives exactly what we want them to be.

If gratitude doesn't come naturally to you, work at it. Post reminders around your home and your car and your office until feeling grateful becomes a habit. You can replace your worry habit (#64) with it.

Get in the habit of taking a few minutes at the end of each day to make a list of all the things that happened that day for which you can be grateful.

You'll find, if you haven't already, there's a self-expansion aspect of gratitude. Very possibly it's a little-known law of nature: the more gratitude you have, the more you have to be grateful for.

83. Take time to think

ONE OF THE frequent reactions I hear from people who've read *Simplify Your Life* has been "It's so obvious what I need to do to simplify. I could have figured out how to do it myself if I'd just *thought* about it."

They're absolutely right. The changes we need to make to our lives are the obvious ones. But we're often too busy to stop and *think* about what we need to do to bring them about. We've been so caught up in the stress and the pressures and the demands of our days that we've gotten out of the habit of thinking about our lives.

As you set out and continue along your path of inner simplicity, be sure to set aside time to think on a regular, even daily, basis. Get in the habit of spending a few minutes in the morning before you start your day thinking about how you want to be in your work and in your interactions with the people you come into contact with.

Then, at the end of the day, take a few minutes to think about how you did in relation to how you wanted to do.

Think about the things that may have kept you from enjoying your day, or from living it the way you'd like to. Then think about how you might do things differently tomorrow.

In addition to the daily evaluations, we need to set aside larger blocks of time to think about the big picture. Use some of your regularly scheduled times of solitude (#93) to really *think* about your inner life and your outer life, where you want to go with each, and what kinds of things you can do to get there.

Set aside time for weekend or longer retreats, and use the time to question your long-accepted assumptions or beliefs. There are few things as liberating as coming up with your own solutions to your own issues.

All the information we need to know about our lives and how to live them is available to us. Thinking is one of the tools we can use to tap into that information.

Inner peace rarely comes about automatically. We have to work at it. Thinking is a powerful tool for that work.

84. Cry a lot

CRYING A LOT is harder than laughing a lot (#59). Crying is discouraged in our culture even more than laughing is. But it's such a powerful tool for clearing out the stuff that gets in the way of our inner growth.

It's possible you need to cry and you're not aware of it. Or maybe you live much of your life on the brink of tears.

In either case, arrange your schedule so you can cry every day for the next week, or however long is necessary. You can do it in the same thirty days you're doing the laughing, or you can do it in the subsequent thirty days. Now that you've simplified your life, you'll have the time.

Allow thirty minutes for the crying; longer if possible. You'll need at least that much time to get the floodgates open. If you get a good cry going, don't stop just because the time is up. Cry to the end of the cry.

As with the laughing, you may need to fake it to begin with. The more drama you can put into it to start with, the better. You may go for several days with only fake tears.

That's all right. Eventually real tears will come. Keep at it until they do.

My friend Cindy recently went through a difficult divorce. She is a strong, mother-earth kind of woman who has spent many years letting everyone else cry on her shoulder. But when it came time for her own tears, she had difficulty in letting them flow.

Finally she started renting tearjerker videos. She would sit in front of the VCR with a box of Kleenex, crying her eyes out, initially over some plot line on celluloid, and eventually over her own life. It took her a couple of months to get through all her tears, but it allowed her to grieve and then released her so she could get on with her life.

We've been told for so long that it's not okay to cry. But it *is* okay. In fact, it's desirable. More than that, it's vital. The energy we've been using to hold back the tears is getting in the way of being who we truly are. Let that energy go, and cry. It'll free you.

Five

Some fun stuff

85. Consult a psychic

SOME PEOPLE WILL no doubt take exception to this suggestion. However, I know from my own experience that a good psychic can provide valuable insights and explanations for our dilemmas when we are unable to come up with them on our own.

Some years ago I found myself in a particularly difficult situation. I was under a lot of stress and simply wasn't able to sort out the problem and move on from it. A good friend called one day with the suggestion that I contact a psychic she knew.

I took her advice and scheduled a psychic reading. Not only did that reading provide a lot of answers for the current situation I was in, and thereby relieve me from a good deal of distress and anguish, but the psychic's comments about what led me to that circumstance, and the probable outcomes, were tremendously helpful in terms of the actions I took for the future.

Many times over the next year or so I read over the notes I kept from our session together, and was continually amazed at the insight and wisdom she had provided. Several times since then I have contacted her on other issues, and found her perceptiveness and clear vision a considerable contribution to my life.

Obviously, this is not to suggest we can turn our lives over to someone else's interpretation of our predicament, no matter how intuitive they are. One's response to a psychic reading should always be coupled with common sense and intelligence.

And now that I've simplified and have created the time to listen, I've made progress in the development of my own insight and intuition. I've reached a point where I can rely on my innate psychic abilities, which we all have—though I wouldn't hesitate to contact a psychic again should the circumstances warrant. I look at it as one more tool we can use to help us gain the insight we may need.

How do you find a good psychic? The same way you find a competent professional in any field: ask around. Interview a few, if necessary, until you find someone you can connect with.

The information we require to solve and understand our own problems is always available to us, but if for some reason we are unable to tap into it on our own, a competent psychic can be a valuable aid in the interim.

86. Cast a rune

ONE FASCINATING AND fun way to get in touch with your intuition is through runes. *The Book of Runes,* by Ralph Blum, can be purchased at most bookstores, along with a bag of twenty-five flat stones roughly the size of a quarter, each imprinted with an ancient Viking symbol. You can easily make your own runes, but you'll want to get Blum's book if casting the runes appeals to you.

Blum's text provides an inspired unconventional interpretation of an ancient alphabetic script that can be used as a contemporary oracle to assist what he calls the Witness Self in dealing with whatever life questions you may find yourself confronted with.

When I first started to experiment with these guides, I was astounded at the accuracy with which my issues were described, and at how appropriate the interpretations were for the situation I was addressing.

My initial thought was that the runes were simply so cleverly written that any one rune pulled could provide answers for any circumstance. Yet, as I look back—I've kept a rune section in my journal for this purpose—I've found a level of relevancy for each individual question that I haven't been able to chalk up simply to good writing. Somehow, the runes always provide just the insight I need at the moment.

I don't know why the runes work and, because they're so easy and so much fun, I really don't care. I've reached the point in my life where, if something works—or even only appears to work—I graciously accept whatever help it can provide.

The runes do not predict the future, nor provide specific advice for one to follow, though they are written with such wisdom that they *seem* to do all this. When you analyze the messages, you see it's your own intuition that pulls what you need from the rune reading for your particular problem at this particular time.

87. Check out subliminal tapes

S EVERAL YEARS AGO a friend gave me a subliminal audiotape for my birthday. It was called "Happiness
and Laughter" and, at her request and to humor her, I kept it
playing softly in an auto-reverse tape player that I kept on my
desk during my work day and in the main part of the house—
or wherever I happened to be—the rest of the time.

My husband Gibbs might accurately be described as a
skeptic. Recognizing this, I didn't bother to mention to him
that the peaceful sounds of nature we were hearing on the tape
were supposedly masking over a million messages per hour
that were recorded on the tape below the conscious level of
hearing.

One morning at breakfast, after about a week of constant
exposure to the subliminal messages on this tape, Gibbs said
to me, "You know, I feel so good. I've never been happier in
my life."

I began to suspect there might be something to subliminal programming. Over the next six months I experimented with more than half a dozen different subjects and brands of tapes.

I haven't explored all the possibilities, but the most effective subliminal tapes I've used are those produced by Alphasonics (35 Cuesta Road, Santa Fe, NM 87505, 1-800-937-2574). I have successfully used their "Stop Procrastination" to get started on the last three book projects I've completed. When it gets down to the wire I pop in "Peak Performance in Business" and am able to work with a level of concentration I haven't yet been able to tap into without the tape.

I played the "I Can Do Anything Tape" for an entire year while I was getting over my fear of public speaking (#51). "Deep Relaxation" got me to a point where I could sit still long enough to begin to learn to meditate. I want very much to try the "Stop Sugar Addiction" tape, but I'm not quite ready to give up Häagen-Dazs Chocolate Chocolate Chip ice cream yet.

In addition to the titles that will assist you in your outer life, there are half a dozen—such as "Joy of Life," "Loving and Feeling Loved," and "Healing Power"—that can help you get started on your inner work.

I don't know for certain how or why subliminal tapes work, but I have found them to be a fun and effective tool for tapping into the power of other levels of consciousness, and a delightful medium for continued growth and change.

88. Stop the world—you *can* get off

SOMETIMES WHEN THE pressures of the world get to be too much, leave it.

Sit quietly wherever you are, close your eyes, breathe deeply for a couple of minutes, and get centered.

Then *imagine* you're on the ceiling, or eight or ten feet above your head. See yourself down below, sitting there quietly, and examine how it feels to have stepped out of your life for a moment. Then go higher, above the rooftops, and look around the town or the countryside. Enjoy the view from this new perspective.

Keep moving higher until you can start to see the curve of the horizon. Everything is below you, except possibly the clouds. You can imagine the people and the traffic down there, you can even hear the faint hum of the collective noises, but you're not part of it for this moment.

Keep moving higher and higher until the earth is a tiny

globe. You are above it all. Free. Enjoy this freedom for as long as you can. Then, when you're ready, gradually return to earth and to your self. *Notice* how you feel and if things *seem* different. Even a slight change can be important for you. The more often you make these smaller changes in your consciousness, the more often you can make larger ones.

89. Write like mad

WHENEVER YOU FIND yourself in a dilemma you don't know how to get out of, or a life situation you simply don't understand, get out some paper and a pen—not your journal, because you're not going to save this or even read it again—and start writing furiously with the hand opposite to your handedness.

Write. Write. Write. Write. Write. Write until you get some relief.

If you're right-handed, writing with your left hand—even though it's harder to do—will help you access your right brain mode at an intuitive level. It will sometimes make it easier to get in touch with your true feelings than when you're using your left-brain analytical mode.

If you find it too difficult to write left-handed, simply write fast and furiously with your right hand, but don't stop to read or analyze what you've written. If you have trouble getting started writing, begin with the Gettysburg Address, and take off from there. Just keep writing until you start addressing the real issue.

Sometimes, when you are under a lot of stress, you're unable to hear messages through your normal channels. Writing like mad is an effective and relatively painless way to access your intuitive wisdom, and to uncover truths previously unknown to you.

90. Chant

CHANTING IS AN ancient and universal practice that has been used in most cultures and in all the major religions of the world as a powerful way to raise consciousness.

This is most effective when done with a group, but chanting can also be done individually to great benefit. Pick an uplifting, soul-expanding word or phrase, in English or any other language, that you respond to.

Sit quietly where you won't be disturbed, and where you won't disturb others. Start repeating your word or phrase out loud. Let a rhythm develop with it. Try several rhythms, until you find one you and your chant can flow with. Clap or sway with it if that feels right. Keep at it until you become one with it, thirty or forty minutes, or however long it takes. This is very uplifting.

Change your word or phrase from time to time. Discover the different properties of each. One might make you peaceful, another might make you happy. Another one might raise your energy. Use your journal to keep track of how you respond to each one.

Then, when you need to change your disposition, pull out the appropriate chant.

91. Dance

FIND A TIME and a place where you won't be disturbed for thirty to forty minutes, or even longer. Wear loose-fitting, comfortable clothes. Put on some music you truly connect with. It can be classical, rock, jazz, drums, whatever. Turn it up as loud as you dare, but not so loud you invade someone else's peace and quiet.

Stand in the middle of the room, close your eyes, and start to feel the music. Let it move through your entire body. Breathe with it. Move your head and arms and your upper body with it. Bend at the waist with it. Still standing in one place, move your feet with it, keeping your eyes closed, sway and gyrate with it, totally absorbing the music into your being.

Slowly open your eyes and start moving around the room with the music. Create your own dance. Whirl and twirl or rock and stomp. Do whatever you need to do to become one with the music. Be totally uninhibited, spontaneous, and ecstatic. It may take you a time or two before you can really let yourself go. Keep at it until that happens.

When the music ends, fall to the floor and lie on your back. Keep your eyes open and gradually, slowly, and with total awareness bring your consciousness back into your body. Stay there absorbing the silence until your breathing returns to normal. Then slowly stand up, and give a slight bow of gratitude to the music and the universe.

Do this every day for a couple of weeks and you will begin to feel incredibly uplifted, lighthearted, and joyous.

If you do this in a group, each person should dance on their own, aware of the others, but not dancing *with* anyone else. A shorter version of this dance is an incredibly enlivening way to begin your inner support group meeting. Or, every now and then, use the entire meeting time to dance.

Six

The real stuff

92. Learn to listen to
your inner voice

I F YOU FEEL you're not naturally intuitive, or if you've lost touch with your inner voice, learning to listen will be a great aid in helping you achieve inner simplicity.

It will require time. It will require patience. It will require discipline. There will be times when you simply have to force yourself to sit still and listen.

Don't forget the listening part. When I first started to work on developing my intuition, I'd ask the questions, but incredibly, I didn't take the time to wait for the answers. Intuitive responses are often quite subtle, especially when we're first learning to tap into them. So unless we're paying close attention, we can easily miss them.

Also, the intuitive *insight* telling you to do something that's easy and that you want to do can be much different from an intuitive *warning* that is urging you to avoid something that might be harmful. Become familiar with how both your body and your mind respond to various situations, and learn to accurately interpret those responses.

Start with the smaller things. Should I turn right at the corner or left? Should I run that errand this afternoon or tomorrow? Should I take the umbrella today or not? Should I make this phone call now or later? There are dozens of times throughout the day when we can ask ourselves these small, seemingly insignificant questions. Every time you find yourself in one of these minor quandaries, ask. Then *listen*.

Use your journal to keep track of the results. If you took your umbrella, did it rain? If you made the call, did it turn out the way you wanted it to? Soon you'll begin to get a sense of what the right answer *feels* like beforehand.

When you've reached a level of certainty about that feeling with the little questions, start asking yourself the bigger ones.

Our explorations of the inner worlds often bring us into exciting and unfamiliar experiences and expose us to new ideas and ways of thinking. There may be times when our habitual methods of responding are no longer appropriate. Learning to interpret your intuitive signals will give you an effective means of examining the old and interpreting the new.

Elsewhere in the book, I've suggested things you might consider doing when your own messages aren't coming through, such as using the runes (#86), or contacting a psychic (#85), or writing like mad (#89). There are many other options as well, such as Tarot cards, the I Ching, using a pendulum, or working with a Ouija board.

If you consult other such oracles, make it a practice to check with yourself first. Then, as you get answers from other sources, check back to see how those answers feel compared to your own. Again, use your journal to help you keep track of these feelings.

The goal is to eventually become familiar with your own responses and begin to rely on them exclusively.

93. Learn to enjoy solitude

T HERE ARE FEW things as powerful as solitude to help you get in touch with your inner self—especially when that solitude is accompanied by silence and the elimination of outside stimuli such as television, radio, newspapers, magazines, and other popular forms of escape.

If you haven't started already, begin to enjoy solitude. Get comfortable with being alone. This is time you can spend on your own thinking, reading elevating stuff, communing with nature, getting in touch with your intuition, smiling, laughing, crying, forgiving, and contemplating the questions of the universe.

This doesn't mean you need to move to a cave in the wilderness. Far from it. People and relationships are a vital part of both our inner and our outer growth. But we all need time to recharge every now and then, not only to nourish our spirit, but so that we have new energy to give to others.

If solitude feels threatening to you, start in small ways, perhaps with a lunch date with yourself in a quiet setting, such as a pew in an open but vacant chapel. Expand that to a Saturday afternoon alone, possibly in a secluded garden or some other place where you won't be disturbed. Then plan a private weekend retreat at home, or possibly in an organized retreat situation where everything but the inner search will be taken care of for you.

Be creative in coming up with ways you can spend time in solitude on a regular basis. I have a friend who for years spent his lunchtime in a deserted cemetery. It was the most convenient quiet place near his office he could find. He claims it got him comfortable not only with being alone, but also with the idea of death, a beneficial concept to have under your belt when you're examining the big issues of your life.

Solitude gives you the opportunity to confront your inner self in ways that few other endeavors can. Out of your times of solitude come serenity, peace of mind, and unparalleled opportunities to connect with your soul.

94. Do nothing

L EARNING TO DO nothing is another valuable tool that will help you get in touch with your inner self. I first learned to do nothing in an attempt to cure myself of the habit of moving too fast, and of trying to do too many things at the same time. And it worked. By *scheduling* time each week to do nothing, I gradually began to get some understanding about where I wanted to go with my professional life.

And as I continued to incorporate this practice into my schedule, I was able to reach a new level of understanding in terms of my inner life as well.

There are plenty of reasons why many of us have been moving at breakneck speed in recent years. Oftentimes, they have nothing to do with trying to accomplish a lot in a short amount of time. Some of us have kept moving, either to prove to ourselves that we're still alive, or in the unconscious fear that if we stop, we'll have to take a close look at who we are. That can be terrifying.

But learning to stop completely can be incredibly constructive. Doing nothing is different from meditating and from spending time in solitude, and in some respects, it is much more difficult. In our culture, anyway, it's usually a learned habit that has to be nurtured. Or sometimes Mother Nature mercifully intervenes by providing us with a convenient ailment that forces us to stop and do nothing.

Accept the fact that it's okay to do nothing. If you've begun to slow down, simplify your life, and go within, doing nothing will be much easier.

You can start by getting in the habit of doing nothing for two to three minutes at various times throughout the day. Simply stop whatever you're doing, sit quietly with your eyes open, your mind aware but not active, and just *be*. Doing some deep breathing (#96) will help.

Gradually increase the time. As you begin to spend more time doing nothing, be prepared for your body or your mind to balk. You'll get hungry or sleepy. You'll think of a dozen things you should be doing or that you think you'd rather be doing. Resist the temptation to give in to those feelings. Think of it as necessary and valuable time, which it is.

When you do this consistently, when you lean into it, when you start to delight in it, you'll find doing nothing one of the most productive inactivities you engage in.

95. Do a retreat

A FORMAL RETREAT can provide an effective jump start for a program of inner simplicity.

A retreat can be as organized or as loosely structured as you wish to make it. If you're just beginning to explore the inner realms, you might wish to spend a few quiet days at a retreat center where you can have time on your own to quietly read and think about your life and where you want to go from here.

In this type of setting, your schedule is completely your own. You don't have to answer to anyone, and there are no ceremonies to attend or rituals to perform, other than ones you might choose. The accommodations vary, but usually a simply furnished room is provided, along with meals—either on your own or in a communal dining room. The general atmosphere is one of quiet reverence that allows for private reflection.

If you're practicing a certain type of meditation, or looking into a new teaching, or even energizing an old one, connecting with a formal retreat center that provides instruction or guidance in the teachings you've chosen to explore might be the way to go.

In this type of arrangement, there is normally a routine the participants are expected to follow as a group, usually with meals together, and with set times for instruction and group discussion, as well as scheduled quiet times during which to practice meditation techniques or other exercises.

Sometimes our expectations can get in the way of having a fruitful experience, so it's helpful to get as much information as possible ahead of time about the setting and particular demands of the routine. Or, at the very least, be willing to change your expectations if necessary. A friend of mine recently attended a four-day retreat to clarify some questions she had about a meditational technique she was learning. Her primary interest was in having a quiet setting, away from traffic and noise.

When she got there, she discovered her room was located directly above one of the major highways of the western world. She seriously considered leaving. But after thinking about it quietly, she decided to go with the flow. The weekend turned out to be incredibly beneficial for her, but completely different from what she had anticipated.

There is an interesting array of retreat experiences available today. If you don't have one in mind, see the reading list for some places to look into.

96. Check your breathing

NCIENT YOGIC TEACHINGS say that if
you can control your breath, you can control your life.
Proper breathing can be an important tool for your inner
growth. It can clear your head, energize your body, raise your
energy, improve your outlook, elevate your mood, restore
your health, rejuvenate your psyche, and take you to other
levels of awareness.

Experiment with your breathing to see what a difference
correct breathing can make in your everyday life.

Yogic breathing involves the use of both the abdomen
and the diaphragm. If you're doing it right, the lungs are filled
with each inhalation and emptied with each exhalation, so
there is no residual air left in the lungs to get stale.

The first thing to do is *get in the habit* of sitting up
straight and standing up straight. The shoulders should be
relaxed and the stomach held in. No slouching towards nir-
vana here.

This also means continually being aware of your level of consciousness. If you're feeling logy, listless, lethargic, down, sleepy, or irritable, it's time to check your breathing.

You can do this by placing your hands lightly on your abdomen, with the fingertips touching. Keep your mouth closed and inhale through the nose, with the area just above the back of the throat actually drawing the breath in. If you exaggerate this step while getting the feel of it, you can hear and feel this as a slight rasp in the back of the throat. Once you're comfortable with the movement, normal breathing should be inaudible.

As you bring the breath in through the nose/throat, the abdomen expands and the bottom of the lungs start to fill with air, followed by the expansion of the rib cage, the top of the lungs, and the upper chest cavity. The fingertips should move apart slightly as the abdomen fills out.

Then gently pull the muscles of the abdomen inward to expel the breath up and out through the abdomen, the chest, and the nose in one smooth movement. The fingertips will come together again.

You can practice lying flat on your back until you get the hang of it. The entire movement for each breath should be fluid and easy. The idea is to have the process be automatic, while at the same time maintaining a level of consciousness with regard to the breath.

Make a point of connecting with your breath throughout the day. Use it to keep yourself on track. The study of hatha yoga is an excellent way to bring the incredible power of the breath into your everyday life.

97. Explore your sleep consciousness

ONE MORNING NOT long ago I found myself totally overcome by drowsiness after having had a rest-
less sleep the night before. When I couldn't keep my eyes
open any longer, I went to bed for a brief nap. I closed my
eyes, and when I became conscious again, in what seemed like
only a few moments, the "I" of me was outside of and hover-
ing above my physical body. I saw and felt a whirling vortex
emanating from the center of my chest.

Before I realized what was happening, the "I" of me was
in the vortex. I sensed rather than heard a pop, and "I" was
back in my body. When I looked at my watch, two hours had
elapsed.

I didn't realize it then, but I'd had an out-of-body experience, commonly referred to as an OBE. Some researchers
suggest we all leave our bodies on numerous occasions during
sleep, though only a very small percentage of us remember

these experiences. Others interpret OBEs as simply another level of dream consciousness. In either case, it would appear we all have the ability to have out-of-body experiences at will.

Why would we want to do this? Well, my own OBE was an incredibly thrilling adventure. It was one of the first times I've had the opportunity to actually *understand* how the "I" of me could be separate from my body, and different from what I'd always felt myself to be. I saw how that "I" of all of us could be eternal and immortal. But most importantly, it has totally expanded my concepts of and beliefs about my life and the possibilities of the universe.

If you've ever done any dream analysis, or taken the time to remember, record, and/or program and direct your dreams, you know that dreams can contribute fascinating and valuable information for our waking lives. Dreams often provide intuitive answers we haven't been able to get from any other source. If we allow them to, dreams can afford a much broader understanding of the greater context in which we live.

Recent research has shown it's possible to learn to control our dreams and to create what we want in our dream life, and then to *transfer* that learning to our waking lives. This offers incredible opportunities for our personal growth.

98. Explore meditation

MEDITATION IS ONE of the most powerful tools we have for self-expansion and inner growth. Through meditation we can reach levels of mental clarity that we cannot achieve through any other means. Meditation is a major pathway to the soul.

There are many, many ways to meditate. You can meditate on the inflow and outflow of the breath. You can meditate using a sacred word or phrase. You can meditate on the flame of a candle, or on the inner light at the center of your forehead.

You can meditate on the idea of love, or wisdom, or immortality, or any other concept. Or you can meditate by simply being aware of your thoughts as they pass through your mind. There are sitting, standing, walking, laughing, crying, dancing, and chanting meditations. There is living your life—every single moment of the day and night—as a meditation. And this is just for starters.

When I first came back to meditation a few years ago

after simplifying my life, I picked up a book on the subject, read through one of the suggested techniques, and sat down to meditate.

When I opened my eyes thirty minutes later, I found myself embraced by one of the most profound feelings of peace and serenity I'd ever known. I recognized in that moment that I'd been given a gift. I knew from my past attempts at meditating that it's not every day that meditation comes so easily, nor are the results so absolute.

It took many more months of regular, dedicated practice of meditation before I encountered even fleeting moments comparable to that initial experience. But I was hooked from that first day, and that was the gift.

Your acquaintance with meditation is no doubt entirely different from mine, or from anyone else's you know. We each bring a unique combination of body, mind, and spirit to the adventure of connecting with our inner selves.

If you haven't explored meditation, I urge you to consider it. Making meditation a regular part of your life will open you up to new and exciting possibilities for your inner growth.

If you don't know where to begin, start with one of the books on the Reading List, and branch out from there. Or connect with a teacher, or contact people you know who have had experience with meditation. If you start now, you will be amazed, when you look back six months or a year from now, at how far you've come and by how much your life has changed for the better. You'll also see how subtly you've been guided through the inner maze.

Meditation provides a natural unfolding of the process of inner exploration. Some of the rewards are immediate. Others take time, often years, to achieve. There is no substitute for simply doing it, and seeing what the rewards are for you.

99. Create joy in your life

A WHILE BACK Gibbs and our little dog, Piper, and I took a stroll down to the beach at sunset. It was one of those spectacular displays that casts a rosy glow, seemingly over the entire creation. There were a few wisps of white clouds in the sky, and as the sun sank lower on the horizon, the clouds became tinged with pink. Within a few moments, they had changed color entirely as they totally absorbed the brilliant hue of the sun. Venus began to be visible in the western sky.

We looked to the east, and saw the nearly full moon rising huge and golden. We sat and watched as the sky changed from one glorious shade to another. We were so enthralled with this exquisite display that we felt nearly full to overflowing with what I can only call unbounded joy.

The next day I found myself starting to succumb to a difficult moment in my work. Perhaps because this irksome note was in such contrast to the continued delight I had been feeling from the previous evening, and because that enjoyment had been so complete, I immediately recalled that sunset. Instantly the difficulty was overshadowed by the re-creation of the joy I'd experienced the night before. It wasn't that I was living in the past, but that I was somehow able to bring that joy to the present.

As the days and weeks passed, I found I was able to tap into that joy again and again, and to absorb it to the present moment. Even now, months later, I'm still getting mileage from that sunset.

We all have these moments in our lives. They are available to us in one degree or another every single day. We can find them in the smile of someone we love, or in the smile of someone we don't even know. We can find them in the hug of a child, in the presence of a friend, or the touch of a lover.

Think about the times in your life when you've been overcome with joy. It's in those moments that you're in love with yourself and everyone else. It's in those moments you believe you can conquer the world. It's in those moments that you dare to imagine how you want your life to be.

It's from that imagination and that belief and that love that we can and do create our lives.

Think about the things that bring you joy, then make a point of connecting with as many of them as possible, as often as possible.

100. Love a lot

L OVE IS THE most important thing in our lives. All the great masters, saints, and sages agree on this. But it seems to me that a lot has been lost in the translation of this teaching. It would appear that many of us have forgotten how to love, or never learned how to love to begin with.

This has always been a difficult issue for me, and I don't claim any expertise here. I've done well—or have been fortunate—when it comes to specific loves, such as my husband and family and friends. But something has always been missing for me when it comes to loving mankind, or the world at large. I believe I've learned one thing about love in recent years, which I'll share with you. For the rest, I'll refer you to the masters.

I've learned that in order to love others, we have to love ourselves first. How do we do that? By allowing ourselves to do things we love to do.

Like many of us, I grew up in a culture that fostered a belief that the most important thing was to get trained for a career so I could support myself and my family. It didn't matter whether or not I liked what I was doing, as long as it paid the mortgage. As a result, I spent years in jobs that drained my energy and starved my spirit.

One of the steps I took to simplify my life was to get to a point where I could do the things I love to do, not only in terms of my career, but in all areas of my life.

Obviously, this is a gradual process, and a lot of the steps I've outlined in this book helped, such as getting counseling, spending time in nature, and figuring out what I *didn't* want, among many others. But having at last found a career in writing and a fulfilling pastime in painting—both of which I love to do—has made all the difference in my ability to share love with the world at large, and to really *feel* that love for others.

If you're feeling weak in the love department, the first place to start is with yourself. Spend some time figuring out the things you love to do, and the things that make you happy. Then start doing them. Don't expect it to happen overnight. It may take you a while, and you might need to get some guidance along the way. Fortunately, there is a wealth of information available today to help you do this.

Many times we've been taught that doing what *we* love to do is selfish or narcissistic. But, in fact, before we can give love to others, we have to fill ourselves with love first.

Reading List

Meditation/Philosophy

Frost, S.F., Jr. *Basic Teachings of the Great Philosophers: Including Plato, Kant, Descartes, Spencer, Rousseau, Comte, Spinoza, Berkeley, Dewey, Santayana, Hegel, Leibnitz, Locke, Aristotle, Bacon.* New York: Anchor/Doubleday, 1942, 1962. Provides a fascinating historical perspective of how our understanding of the universe and a higher power has developed through the centuries, and continues to develop and unfold.

Hittleman, Richard. *Guide to Yoga Meditation: The Inner Source of Strength, Security, and Personal Peace.* New York: Bantam, 1969. A good beginning guide to hatha yoga and meditation.

Levine, Stephen. *A Gradual Awakening.* New York: Anchor/Doubleday, 1979. For those already familar with meditation and looking for new areas to explore.

Lindbergh, Anne Morrow. *Gift from the Sea.* New York: Vintage Books, 1978. A charming story of one woman's search for solitude and simplicity and the meaning of life.

Snow, Kimberly, Ph.D. *Keys to the Open Gate: A Woman's Spiritu-*

ality Sourcebook. Berkeley, CA: Conari Press, 1994. A collection of spiritual insights, meditations, and experiences from numerous classic and contemporary sources.

Strong, Mary. *Letters of the Scattered Brotherhood: A Twentieth-Century Classic for Those Seeking Serenity and Strength*. San Francisco: HarperCollins, 1991. This is a soothing companion to have in times of stress, anger, frustration, worry, loneliness—or any time. It offers page after page of practical guidance and inspiration about how to move beyond the distractions of the day and create inner peace.

Retreats

Benson, John. *Transformative Adventures, Vacations & Retreats: An International Directory of 300+ Host Organizations*. Portland, OR: New Millennium Publishing, 1994.

Cooper, David A. *Silence, Simplicity, and Solitude: A Guide for Spiritual Retreat*. New York: Bell Tower, 1992. An exquisitely simple and readable description of how to prepare for and what to expect from a spiritual retreat.

Ram Dass. *Journey of Awakening: A Meditator's Guidebook*. New York: Bantam, 1990. A good general guide for launching a spiritual quest. Includes a directory of retreat centers and groups that teach meditation and provide retreat accommodations.

Sadleir, Steven S. *The Spiritual Seeker's Guide: The Complete Source for Religions and Spiritual Groups of the World.* Costa Mesa, CA: Allwon Publishing Co., 1992.

Health/Exercise/Love/Healing

Anderson, Bob. *Stretching.* Bolinas, CA: Shelter Publications, 1980. Outlines various stretching programs for keeping your body limber.

Chopra, Deepak, M.D. *Perfect Health: The Complete Mind Body Guide.* New York: Harmony Books, 1990. An excellent program for physical, mental, and spiritual health.

Jonas, Steven, M.D., and Radetsky, Peter. *PaceWalking: The Balanced Way to Aerobic Health.* New York: Crown, 1988. A healthful alternative to running or jogging.

Siegel, Bernie S., M.D. *Love, Medicine & Miracles: Lessons Learned About Self-Healing from a Surgeon's Experience with Exceptional Patients.* New York: Perennial Library/Harper & Row, 1986.

———. *Peace, Love & Healing: Bodymind Communication & the Path of Self-Healing: An Exploration.* New York: Perennial Library/Harper & Row, 1989. As Bernie Siegel's books illustrate, we can and do heal ourselves.

Creativity/Affirmations/Visualizations/
Exploring Other Levels of Consciousness

Cameron, Julia. *The Artist's Way: A Spiritual Path to Higher Creativity.* Los Angeles: Jeremy P. Tarcher, 1992. This program will free you to develop your own creative process.

Ferrucci, Piero. *What We May Be: Techniques for Psychological and Spiritual Growth through Psychosynthesis.* New York: Tarcher/Perigee, 1982. Provides many easy mind-expanding techniques for exploring other levels of consciousness.

Gawain, Shakti. *Creative Visualization.* New York: Bantam, 1983. A beginning guide to affirmations and visualizations.

Silva, Jose, with Philip Miele. *The Silva Mind Control Method.* New York: Pocket Books, 1989. How to use affirmations, visualizations, and the alpha level of the mind to help you arrange your life exactly as you want it to be.

Sleep/Dreams/Out-of-Body Experiences

Godwin, Malcolm. *The Lucid Dreamer: A Waking Guide for the Traveller Between Worlds.* New York: Simon & Schuster, 1994. A beautifully illustrated and written exploration of the world of dreams.

LaBerge, Stephen, Ph.D. Stanford University Sleep Research Center. *Lucid Dreaming: The Power of Being Awake & Aware in Your Dreams.* New York: Ballantine, 1985. Dr. LaBerge's work has brought much-needed understanding and insight to the study of dreaming.

Stack, Rick. *Out-of-Body Adventures: 30 Days to the Most Exciting Experience of Your Life.* Chicago: Contemporary Books, 1988. A straightforward, proven approach for anyone interested in exploring out-of-body experiences.

I would love to hear about any steps you might be taking to achieve inner simplicity. Please send to

Elaine St. James
c/o Hyperion
114 Fifth Avenue
New York, NY 10011